From

PIMPIN' *to the* PULPIT

Saved from horror to heaven

REVEREND. JAYMES BROWNE

Copyright © 2014 by Reverend. Jaymes Browne

From Pimpin to the Pulpit
Saved from horror to heaven
by Reverend. Jaymes Browne

Printed in the United States of America

ISBN 9781498406604

All rights reserved solely by the author. The author guarantees all contents are original and do not infringe upon the legal rights of any other person or work. No part of this book may be reproduced in any form without the permission of the author. The views expressed in this book are not necessarily those of the publisher.

Scripture quotations taken from the New International Version (NIV). Copyright © 1973, 1978, 1984, 2011 by Biblica, Inc.™. Used by permission. All rights reserved.

Scripture quotations taken from the Contemporary English Version (CEV). Copyright © 1995 American Bible Society. Used by permission. All rights reserved.

www.xulonpress.com

I want to say at the outset that I have become ill and insane as an inmate of the torture chamber behind America's fake façade of justice and democracy but I'm not as ill as I was and I'm getting better all the time.

I want to make it clear that my reason for starting these notes at a point of personal anguish and suffering is that these experiences marked the end of a corrupt pimp life and were the prelude to a still mauled but constructive new life.

FROM PIMPIN'

A pimp is happy when his ladies are giggling. He knows that they are still asleep...all ladies have one thing in common just like the chumps who are humping for their white bosses. It thrills them when a pimp makes a mistake. They watch and wait for his downfall.

TO THE PULPIT

1a. A raised platform or high lectern from which a clergyman preaches in a church.

(Neh8:4)
(4)And Ezra the scribe stood upon a pulpit of wood, which they had made for that purpose; and beside him stood Mattithiah, and Schema, and Anaiah, and Uriah, and Hilkiah, and Messiah, on his right hand; and on his left hand, Pedaiah, and Michael, and Malachi, and Hashbadana, Zechariah, and Meshullam.

By Rev. Jaymes Browne

TABLE OF CONTENTS

From Pimpin' - To The Pulpit............................ vii

Introduction xi

Pastoral Preface................................... xvii

1. One, two, three and to the four, we're at the door................................... 19
2. First Steps into the Game.................... 32
3. "It's all about the money. The money gets the honey" 56
4. Dale tells the real deal on how they met...... 68
5. "I Had To Stop Her" 85
6. The Down Fall 99
7. "It All Went Down Hill from Here" 102
8. "This is where my life was about to turn around."............................ 107
9. "California Here I Come" 110

10. "The Dust Bowl" 114
11. Yo! World! " I'm on my way back" 117
12. "Another life Speed Bump" 121
13. "Away We Go" 128
14. "The Lord Is Giving Me another Chance" 139
15. "Everything That Looks Good...." 142
16. "Here We Go Again" 148
17. "Why Can't I Do the Right Thing" 152
18. "Falling On My Face Again" 159
19. "I Can't Do This Again" 167
20. ARE YOU READY? 183
21. Back to the sermon /testimony 186
22. Being someone that God can use 191

My Dear Brothers and Sisters 193

INTRODUCTION

This is the voice of Rev. Jaymes Browne

It is by God's Grace that I am afforded this opportunity to address you...

My name is Jaymes Browne, my street name was Jay Bee and my state number is 943241. I will attempt to take you on a short trip into a world that many may enter but few ever return from, an underworld of Darkness and a maze of Deceptions in a world of lost hopes.

A world where your dreams can come true then evaporate into thin air.

A world where you can take the easy way out and this delighted me that I was defying and trampling upon the man's law, upon his system of values and that I was defiling his women.

From Pimpin to the Pulpit

My Brothers and Sisters, I am talking about a world that is so dark and ugly that the only light at the end of the tunnel is Death or the light of the Gate Keepers (the Parole Board). Through this door is your only hope to the world of light. Some may think that they can pimp and rule in this world forever, that's a lie.

Of three boys and one girl, I had all the opportunities my parents could afford and even went to college for a while but left when I found an easier way to make money fast.

I have been a Pimp, a Drug Dealer, a Drug User, a Thief, and a woman abuser /user. These were the tools that I used to enter this Underworld of Darkness.

Introduction

You see, being a pimp will only lead you to two places, death or a place where the laws of humanity do not apply when it comes to this world.

Once we enter this world, we are placed in a holding facility, much like a dog pound, called the "County Jail."

This is a place where they cram at least three men in a cell that was originally made for one person. Yes, even I have slept under a urinal for months and have caught boils and rashes. I have even slept on the floor in the so-called day room for days where the dust is so thick it's like crossing a desert. We are fed just enough food to survive and if we voice our opinion about any problems, we are not given the choice to have a witness of our own choosing to be present during questioning.

Communication through the mail is mysteriously stopped at times so that we cannot alert any one on the outside until the problems are fixed.

I am sure that everyone knows that tampering with the mail is a Federal Offense, but in this world, the chain has a weak link. In other words, NO ONE gives a damn! You see, we are placed on top of one another like the slaves on a slave ship bound for the so-called free world. In other words, we were being treated as if we were lower than dirt. These are just some of the inhuman living conditions in this world.

This is what you should know! Behind these (concentration camp) walls, everything imaginable happens. There are inmate trustees who are given a little freedom to come and go as they please, but all of them take their jobs to the extreme by turning into the jail house snitches, thinking they are owners of the extra food trays or anything else that is not nailed down. They say that they even own the women who are housed in the same facility.

They say, "I saw her first," not thinking about how horrible she looks when she gets up in the morning. Ha, ha, ha, you see, they argue about every little thing from potato chips to popcorn to you got more food on your tray than I do and even the damn TV. (The TV is just another way to keep everyone asleep.) From the ages of 19 to 50 years old, they argue about Dragon Ball Z. I know what you are thinking! And yes, it is sad, but true! If you do not know, then you will now begin to know because pimpin' ends up in a place like this.

In here, when you are in the middle of throwing up or even in the bathroom urinating or even defecating,

Introduction

you must cut it short. Why, because, you are owned by the State. Everyone has a number, even you. You see, in here you must stop what you are doing and get on line for count time.

Being one of the greatest pimps ever, I have had the opportunity to go into the woman's pod. You see, I waxed floors at night and on one of those nights while I was working, I heard whispering behind me, so I turned around and there stood five officers and two sergeants and they had blackjacks and everything they needed to stop a small platoon, but what stood out was the fifteen pound container of mace. To make a long story short, they went into the pod (cellblock) and came out with a seven foot tall, 120-pound woman and to me she looked like Queen Nefertiti. (Boy, I wish I had her on the streets) Now mind you, all of the seven CO's were over 220-pounds and they only came out with one woman, and when it was all over, I was told to go inside to clean up. Now all of the women were locked in cells, even four to a cell. Only one cell was destroyed! Now what does that tell you? Seven on one, did they do a hell of a job or did they just "cop a feel?"

Did you know that when an inmate/jail house pimp is doing something constructive or even singing to pass the time away, even while they are working, there is always a corrections officer or another inmate to bring you down. Now I can understand that it is a CO's job to first use verbal force if there is a problem. Hell I did the same thing with my girls but there are many scared punks who unnecessarily go beyond the call of being a parasite. (One who sucks the life out of the dead) Parasites and correction officers are the same.

Now when an inmate/jail house pimp does not accept the reality of being in jail, then he becomes a parasite. Then there are inmates/jail house pimps who cannot do quiet time and just go home! You know what I mean! The ones who can't just do their time and go home are part of the purposely mis-educated. (They don't know who they are anymore.) They will take from anyone who shows weakness, your peace of mind, your money, even your sex. You see, there are many fools who need attention just to make it in jail, even if it means putting their own lives in danger.

The week before going in front of the Parole Board, I prayed. Now you might ask, so what's the big deal about praying? Well, in this world I was too ashamed to get down on my knees and pray. "Getting down on my knees was something that I had to really pray about." The only way that you would pray in here is to belong to the Muslims but the week before Parole, I said, "the hell with it" because I want to go home and would have done anything.

PASTORAL PREFACE;

From Bishop James Washington
<u>The New Shiloh Baptist Church</u>

I want to thank Rev. Browne for his brutally honest commentary on his life; Before Christ and since Jesus has come into his life.

For some of you it may be difficult to see Grace and Mercy in his statements. Yet, I thank the Lord that this testimony is proof positive of the power of God to save, from the gutter most to the uppermost.

Rev. Browne has been a great servant of the Lord, in taking care of the Lord's Under-Shepherd and serving the Ministry of Shiloh Church.

There are probably many more of you, with untold stories of being saved from Horror to Heaven.

It is my prayer that we learn that the Lord is no respecter of person's. Then we can begin to go everywhere; even to those in the "red-light district" with the light of the Gospel....Bishop James Washington.

In closing, I just want to leave a reminder that every time someone commits a crime, God finds a witness, but some like to call him or her a snitch!

<u>*By Rev. Jaymes Browne*</u>

CHAPTER ONE

ONE, TWO, THREE AND TO THE FOUR, WE'RE AT THE DOOR
READY TO MAKE AN ENTRANCE, SO BACK ON UP, CAUSE YOU KNOW WE'RE ABOUT TO RIP YOUR WORLD UP.

It was June 2006 and the sermon I gave in church had given me such a spiritual high that left me breathless.

I could still hear the echoes of praising in my ear from the saints who were filled with the Spirit of God.

As I entered my office, full of exhilaration, there was a young man sitting in my office with his head bent down. He had made an appointment with me after hearing me speak at the Rescue Mission.

As I walked in I said "whaz-up man?" extending my hand to shake. This is my second time in your church Rev. and I really like your services. After taking off my jacket and examining the man, I leaned back in my leather recliner. "So what can I do for you? "

Rev. I just got off of parole and things are hard out here. I'm trying to go straight, but shit, oh excuse me, things is hard. I said, "Look man, talk to me like you feel it." Ok, anyway I went to jail for some dumb shit that some hood rat said I did. I didn't do nothing wrong. WORD!

As he paced the floor wearing a tan suit, about 19 years old, a killer look in his eyes, he had a look of defeat. His swagger was that of a jail house thug and a punk. During the time that he was pacing, I tried to think of his name but I was having a senior moment. Finally it hit me. His name was Ricky B. from the Rescue Mission.

"Anyway Rev., I was thinking about being a pimp, that way I can use all them so-call bitches that are always trying to run game on a player. It's get back time for them ho's that got me busted, know what I mean? I'll be the badest pimp ever. I'm gonna have money, I'm gonna have big ass cars, spending a grand at the bar, while kicking it with them hood superstars. Can you feel me Rev?"

"Man! You young guys don't know nothin' about pimpin'." The game has changed, but the rules are still the same. I should know because I used to be one of the top pimps out of Atlantic City. No nigga could touch me back in the day."

"Shit, you were a pimp Rev?" I can't believe it, a pimp turned into a preacher. Ain't that some shit?" he smirked.

Since I was just a boy, I punished ho's with a sick joy. For pimpin', I've been to the joint and heard a shrink say "son, it appears to me that you hate your daddy". "Doc, I pleaded. I just want to be fair. Can't I make it up somewhere? He sighed, you've mugged his heart. You've lived like Satan's pet. I bet nobody can pay a daddy's debt."

Man-o-Man, I could hear my skull yelling please take me back to my cell where I was winding up a 3 year bid.

Have a seat, my brother, and let me rap to you a bit about the pimp game.

You see "I won the highest honors given to a pimp. No one could touch me when I was on top of my game." I smiled and glanced at a picture of me holding my trophy at the player's ball dressed in my fur Chinchilla coat and matching hat.

The day I got the call was the happiest day in my life. I immediately recognized the voice on the phone as that of my man Honey Brown. "What's up man?" I shouted. Honey was shouting, "Nigga, you sittin' down for the news?" "What news y'all talking about?" Honey Brown's voice resonated through my body when he gave me the information. "You won, Jay Bee," he yelled. "What the hell y'all talking about, nigga?" "You're player of the year, pimp!" And as he was talking my mine was racing like crazy.

I didn't know what to think or how to act. Shit, I was chosen for the badass pimp award. It takes hard work to get to that level. They judge you on all kinds of shit. How many bitches you have on the stroll, how much cash you made in a year, getting respect all over the states and how you handle your business. I was running shit, I thought to myself. "Thanks man for telling me. I have two weeks to get ready for the ball and shit." I was caught up in the moment when Ricky started laughing. "I still can't believe what you're telling me. Most preachers don't tell about their past.

" You got my respect Rev. I heard about the Player's ball. Only real pimps heard about the ball."

"I can tell you all about the Players Ball. There was nothing like it. It's like winning an academy award for hustlers. Winning the Player's Ball earned you respect from all the players in the street. You were a celebrity, walking down the carpet, only it was green for the money."

"There were two weeks of preparation for the "Player's Ball". My boys, their women and I took a working trip to New York City. All the pimps and ho's shopped over top of Nathan's hot dog shop where there was a room full of pool tables with everything you could imagine, from fur coats, minks, dresses, tailored suites and jewelry. If there was something you wanted from a booster they could go into any store and get it for you at discount prices. I had a black and gray pinstriped tuxedo made and a white ruffle shirt, with black and gray ostrich shoes to match for my grand entrance for the ball. I had my white fur chinchilla coat. I had to outdo everyone."

Ricky looked at me with awe. "Rev., you must have been the man. "What was the ball like?" he asked smiling proudly.

My ladies had the night off and I made sure they came dressed in the finest clothes. I went all out and brought four fur coats with matching muffs. My girls came in top class riding in a white stretch limo. I came in a horse and buggy with the tap player blowing out James Brown's, "It's a Man's World." I didn't want to drive in a car because the police and feds were out, taking pictures of license plates and snapping all kinds of pictures. You see, I always stayed one step ahead of the game.

The driver opened the door to the carriage while I stood by the door waiting for my ladies to get out of the limo. They waited by the curb until I gave the signal for them to start walking. I nodded my head and they followed behind me. The bright lights were positioned on the green carpet. The photographers were taking pictures. The pimps were dressed in their best suits and hats with their furs. Everyone was a celebrity; it was the ghettos Oscar night for the players and pimps. As I walked down the green carpet with my ladies walking behind me, a pimp from Florida by the name of "Gator," looked at me with a look of disdain on his face. I thought to myself. "I hope this nigga wasn't going to start any gangster shit tonight."

The night I won, I was riding high. Gator came in third place and another pimp from New York named Christopher came in second. "That was the biggest night in my life", I said reflecting on my pimping days.

Ricky looked at me like I was a star. "You really were a true pimp. You must've had it made and shit. It's hard tryin' to survive on these streets. You had it sweet," Ricky said taking in the excitement from the conversation.

"It wasn't always sweet; sometimes when being a pimp you can experience some hard shit on those streets." Like one day I was at this hospital in Camden standing at the bedside of one of my ladies. She had more tubes and shit strapped to her body then a V8 engine and a huge machine was pumping away. I was scared as shit standing there watching her lay helplessly in bed. She spoke in a whisper with her hand balled in a knot covered in blood. She came to the hospital cut up by a trick in Philadelphia.

She was left for dead and it had me shittin' in my pants. I walked over slowly as my heart began to race out of control. She opened her hand and there was the color of green covered in blood. Shit I said to myself. This is the money that she owed me from her nights work. I snatched the money and took off down the long corridor. I didn't look back. I didn't want any cops questioning me like I had something to do with this shit.

I drove my caddy back to Atlantic City. A couple days later on the street I heard that she had died. I didn't have time for that sentimental bull shit. I had ladies on the street and money to be made.

Ricky looked at me with a look of pride. "Shit Rev., you been through some shit. I mean stuff," he boasted.

"You ain't heard nothin' yet. This is only a portion of what my life used to be. I'm lucky to have come out alive. I saw many of my friends die on the street."

Ricky was so into my story that I decided to close it down for now. I told him that I had to meet my wife so lets' pick it up next week. We shook hands and he left with a smile

As I was sitting there with my feet on my desk, hands folded in back of my head and eyes closed, my mind begin to think back to the real stuff that went on back in the day.

One of the first things that flashed in my mind was "Little Bit". She was a black 21 year old with a body by Fisher and a mind by Mattel. I had copped her from a pimp name Wayne in Atlantic City and took her with my other ladies to work in New York. Although she made good money, she would always try to start some kind of shit just to get her ass kicked.

You see, she liked for me to kick her ass. She got off like that. Anyway, one night when all the girls were getting ready for work I was tired and laying on the bed when she came into the bed room with a hair brush in her hand. She put the brush in my hand and with her hand still on it and started to beat herself upside her head. I turned to her and in a sleepy voice said "look babe, if you crack a couple grand tonight, I will have a big surprise for you." Well, when I went to check her trap, she had about $5000.00 dollars.

To keep my word, I went down to the Village in New York and bought a cat-of-nine-tails whip and two sets of hand cuffs.

I drove to this spot under the Brooklyn Bridge that used to be a parking lot. It had a chain link fence that wrapped around the whole parking lot. I had her to strip down in the car, and then I handcuffed her to the fence and started to beat the hell out of her back. Her big ass was now so sweaty and bloody that it shined like a new black Cadillac under the light of the moon. After about 5 minutes my dick started to get hard.

That's when I got scared. My mind was playing tricks on me. Paranoia set in. All I could think of was, "this ain't my kind of shit." I kept thinking that any minute now the cops would show up and hear her screams of enjoyment and want to handcuff my ass to the fence and beat me. So I took her back to the hotel room to get cleaned up. In the meantime, I went to the other girls rooms, packed up all their shit, got in the car and went to check the rest of my traps. After picking up the rest of the girls and making sure that my money was right, we headed back to AC. I often wondered what happened to "Little Bit."

Ring, Ring, Ring! The phone was ringing, I almost fell out of my chair as I picked up the phone and said hello! And the voice on the other end was my wife Dale,

One, two, three and to the four, we're at the door

asking if I had forgotten to pick her up from work. I jumped up and went to pick her up. While driving to pick Dale up, an old song by the Persuasions was playing on my CD. Immediately, I thought I should have told Ricky about the time that I was locked up.

You see in the cold-blooded academy of the ghetto streets, I was taught early that suffering is inevitable and necessary for an aspiring pimp.

I learned also that sympathy is a counterfeit emotion for suckers. Anyway while locked up within the moldering walls of Atlantic County Jail, in one of its cell houses where rows of steel punishment cubicles where rule breaking inmates spend at most 5-7 hours a day. Dale was outside looking at me like she was going to kick my ass for being late. She got in the car and we started home. I went back to thinking about when I was locked-up!

I was locked in one of the steel boxes for over a year, waiting to go to court on a pimp charge. (When I was in California this pretty white girl had chose me, I didn't know that she was a crack head so one night after messing up my money, I had to put my pimp foot in her ass. To make a long story short, she went to the police and put a pimp charge on me). Even now, a new life and a few decades later, I will lay odds that until the grave the images and sounds of that violent, gibbering year will stomp and shudder through my mind.

One instance, among many, I was in a pleasant mood when I hear through a window in my cell door the everyday bull shit in the steel box next to mine. It was my only pimp buddy "Dante" from L.A. He was chanting freaky lyrics of a crazy frightening song about how God is a double crossing cocksucker and how he is going to sodomize and murder his crippled bitch mama.

I cried out like a scolded child leaping off my mattress and stood on trembling legs peering into Dante's cubicle through a ragged break in the weld of the sheet steel wall. He's buck naked and his soft black baby face is twisted hard and hideously as he stands slobbery with his hands flying like some frenzied bats up down his long stiff penis.

I'm thinking that he's trying to run some kind of game on the guards for some personal benefit or advantage.

But there's a chilling realism, perfection about Dante's awful performance, so I tried to talk to him gently.

One, two, three and to the four, we're at the door

"Yo, Dante. Put your pants on man and stop that bullshit. Those ass kickers will show up any minute and by the time you get to the hospital they will have fucked you up. Straighten up man, do it for me, pal. Come on man, you know that I have a weak stomach." This fool gives me a zero response and his walling eyes are like the high beams on a mack truck. I felt a jolt of panic in my chest and a terrifying fluttery quaking inside my skull.

And because I know that madness can be catching, I get real stupid and scream, "You little bitch. You're supposed to be a player, remember? What you gonna' do, let these assholes come and fuck you up?"

But he was so pitiful that I went soft on him and tried to plead with him. "Dante, please man. Get your shit together. Please man, listen to me!"

I begged him until I stank of emotional sweat and my voice faded to a squeaky whisper. But Dante couldn't hear me or anything else except his own hellish drum beat. Finally, the guards come to take Dante away forever and now he's yelping and whimpers like a little puppy under their fists and feet. I was quivering and my teeth slashed into my bottom lip with every kick. While Dante was being dragged away, I fell to the concrete floor and rolled myself into a fetal ball holding my head.

The tragedy of Dante and its recurring long range misery for me is but one "house of horror" among many that haunt my new life today.

A day or so before my expected legal release date from this "Hell House", I got the word that Dante was moved to South Woods and was now crazy as hell.

I had survived and thank God, I would be escaping this steel box within forty eight hours, "because the bitch that tried to fuck me with this shit never showed up to court and the police couldn't find her."

But suddenly I was terrified at the prospect of freedom. Almost immediately I realized why. I was caught in this nightmare that all older pimps face after the age of thirty five. This shit had set me so far back. I had lost all of my pimping tools like my out-of-sight car, my wardrobe, and my diamonds. All the tools that a pimp needs to hook and enslave a fresh stable of humping young whores. My Bottom or main lady had chosen another pimp from Boston and gave him all my shit.

How was I going to make it out there in the free world with no training except in the art of pimping?

I vowed that I would kill myself before I became like "Pretty Eddie." He had been one of the biggest pimps that I had idolized as a boy when I was getting my PHD from S.W.U. (Side Walk University)

It was a hot summer afternoon in New York at the peak of my pimping and I was confronted on the sidewalk outside my hotel by an old black man. He had an old ragged shoeshine box and he stank like he had shit on himself.

I declined a shine but his face was like a ghost inside my head. Almost mechanically, I gave him a twenty dollar bill and went past him. His face haunted me across a dozen states and cities.

Six months later I was smoking some crack in a pimp's crib. An old whore was there all fucked up and was talking about how much money she had made for her pimp "Pretty Eddie" and what a helluva pimp he had been. And then suddenly I knew who that filthy old bum with the shoeshine box was.

Well, they released me and as I stood weakly outside the joint at the bus stop, blinking in the April sun, I was confused and just a shadow of my old self unsure of what direction Atlantic City was. I chose a direction and found freedom from the box so intoxicating that I walked miles before my legs got rubbery and thank God a bus was now coming, Thank you Jesus!

Once in A.C., I got off on M.L.K. and went to a barber shop on Atlantic Avenue. I had expected the barber to perform a minor miracle but his mirror told me that I looked like my own grand pop.

Dale yelled "JAY BEE! What's wrong with you? We just passed the house. Are you day- dreaming or is something wrong with you?" I said "My Bag!"

Once we got home, Dale went into the kitchen and started to cook some chili, so I went to my home office to check on my e-mails and Farmville on Face Book.

After an hour or so on the computer, I decided to lay down for awhile since Dale was cooking.

After a few minutes my eyes started to close, and again my mind drifted to a time when I would have done anything to live the life of my heroes, like Super Fly, The Mack, and all the pimps from New York, Florida, Chicago, and California.

CHAPTER 2

FIRST STEPS INTO THE GAME

I guess my trip downward really was cinched when I was working for the Italians. My best friend, Cliff's father was in the Mob. He set us up with running errands and picking up money from a whore house on Georgia Ave.

I was with my homeboy Cliff, heading to one of the most famous nightclubs owned by the gangsters of Atlantic City. My best friend and his family were tight with the mob. In fact, my best friend's father was a made-man. That was a high position. It was like being CEO of a major firm and shit. Cliff's family had money to spend and he did not spare any expense in sharing some of the money. Me, I didn't have any money to share. My folks worked hard and we didn't have a big house but we managed.

It was a privilege, a black man at seventeen being invited to the 500 club. My knees nearly gave in as I walked in back of Cliff. "What you so nervous about?" Cliff asked. "Relax, man nobody's gonna do anything to you." "I'm cool, just a little nervous. I heard so many

First Steps into the Game

things on T.V. about gangsters taking people out and you never see them again." There was this uneasiness in my voice as I said that I didn't wanna be the cause of any trouble. Cliff walked in like he was a regular. There were three men huddled in a far corner of the room. It was dim, which made it hard to focus.

One of the men was heavy set, like he wouldn't hesitant to pop your ass at a moments' notice. There was also a thin man with a stern look on his face. He looked at us and said,

"Cliff! Hello my boy," he smiled giving him a bear hug. "How's your dad. I'm proud of him making it. He deserved it. How are things in school?""Not bad, but I wanna make some real money now.""Stay in school, the thin man said and get an education.""Who's this?" He asked looking me over. "This is my best friend, Jay Bee.""Hello boy! My name is "Vinnie". Any friend of Cliff's is a friend of ours." At that moment I felt a sense of tension rise from my shoulders. I had no fears. Cliff's Italian background and his father's connections made me important.

Come over here fellows and meet some of the crew, he said pointing to the men at the table. This is "Mickey and Tony." "What's happening fellows?"As we ordered sodas from the bar and sat with the men, we ran down our ideas for over an hour. "I tell you what, Jay Bee. You can run some of our errands and we'll pay you. How would you like that?"I was tongue tied, not knowing what to say.

Here these guys are rolling in money and power and I'm sitting' inside one of the most prestigious clubs in Atlantic City—The 500 club was the spot, next to the Club Harlem.

"I'll do whatever you need, Vinnie." Cliff smiled and nodded his head. "That's great." Cliff said "Thanks, Vinnie." "No problem, anything for family."

The following week I was doing small errands for the Guineas. I went for their cigarettes and other items they might need. I was paid one hundred dollars a day for my hard work. I was riding high with this kind of money in my pockets. You couldn't tell me I didn't have money.

After having a taste, I didn't want to go back to being broke. It's something about the smell of green that leaves you with a taste for wanting more. I thought about my plans with Cliff and how we could make more money. After I got a run down on the Chez Paree Club from Cliff, I was excited to bring him the idea of us running the club. Cliff would bring the idea to his father.

The following day Cliff and I went to his father's house trying to persuade him to let us run the club. Cliff and I had big ideas of making lots of cash.

We didn't give a fuck about college, but that was the right thing to do at the time, I wanted fast money. I had no time to wait for the end of four years to possible make a decent living. Cliff felt the same as I did, so we decided to shoot the idea past his Father about managing the club. Cliff's father, Tony had connections with his contracting business. He had money and power.

We walked into the living room. The house had five bedrooms and a large back yard big enough to build another house. The living room had a handmade Italian sofa. There were expensive paintings and antiques scattered throughout the house. We walked into the family room that had a pool table and a bar in the back of the room. The house had hard wood floors with a shine that was brilliant. Cliff's Father came into the room, and said "what's up boys?" So Cliff and I ran down our plans for the club. Of course he had a million questions for us but for the love of his son he said "OK."

About 3 months later, you guessed it. The music was loud enough to be heard a block away from New York Ave. I was in my glory. Cliff and I were managing one of the most famous nightclubs, courtesy of my homeboy's father and the Italians.

I walked around the club sporting my cream color tailor made suit with leather shoes to match. I exuded style and grace. I was slowly building up my confidence with the women. And that was about to change.

She was tall with tits that jumped at you at attention. She was so tan that I had to look twice to see if she was a sister. She wore a tight fitting red dress with shoes to match. She stopped in front of me and smiled. "Hello there," she said in a soft tone. She flipped her hair in my face. I inhaled smelling the sweet scent of her hair which reminded me of strawberries and cream. I smiled and nodded my head. "I hear you have a nice club here," she said moving in closer to me rubbing her tits on my chest. "This is for you," the woman said handing me a small box. "This is something for you because you're so nice." I took the box and smiled. "I have to go. Things are getting busy around here. I'll catch up with you later."

I made my way to the bar to inspect the liquor. Then I checked out the bouncer. His name was Jimmy Hood. He was about the size of Mike Tyson with muscles. He took care of any problems that the club encountered. There was one time when Jimmy had to break up a fight. He literally beat the hell out of both men and threw them out to the boardwalk.

Everyone feared Jimmy. He had the look of death in his eyes and a heart of stone. He wouldn't hesitant to give anyone a beat down. "You gonna pass up that pussy?" Jimmy said. "Man if that was me, I would take her in the office and get busy." I said, "Man, she thinks like all white women that black men are packing big dicks." He grinned. "You need to prove her right, Jay."

I started sweating and wiped my brow. "I will in time." I had to take it easy. I was not used to women giving me that much attention. Being a light skinned black man put me at an advantage, especially managing a popular night club. I had to admit to myself that I never had but one woman and I felt like a virgin.

I walked around feeling proud about our recent accomplishments with the club in such a short time. This was an opportunity of a lifetime for me being a young black man. The crowd poured in like a running faucet mixed with mostly whites. The blacks had their entertainment on Kentucky Avenue.

There was Club Harlem and the many bars and night spots there. The street was bright with its shining lights and fancy cars parked along the streets. A few blacks would venture to New York Avenue. That was where the gay crowd hung out.

I went to the office to see my partner and best friend Cliff, who was counting the stacks of cash with a wide grin on his face. "Jay we're rolling in dough man. I think we hit over our marker. Friday and Saturday we brought in eight grand, including the sale from the liquor." He raised his hand gesturing for me to give him a high five.

"That's what I am talking about money." I said, taking a seat in front of the desk. The mini room did not hold much but a black desk and two chairs. There was a safe built into the wall which the guineas made sure was secure. They had information in the safe on just about everybody in Atlantic City Government.

Cliff and I had a heads up on the daily operation of the Italians running Atlantic City. Politicians and cops were on the payroll. They controlled trash routes, prostitution and drugs.

"Look at this money, we have more than we hoped for," Cliff said trying to break my concentration. "You alright man, look at this beautiful sight of green," Cliff boasted loudly. "We have money and next the women will be lined at our feet, begging for our dicks."

I laughed and stood up looking in awe at the money. "We're bringing in more than we expected. I think our cut should go up. Talk to your father and Vinnie and tell them that we are doing damn fine," I said proudly.

I reached into my pocket and pulled out a fancy gold watch. "Look at what that girl in the red dress gave me. You remember the Italian one with the big tits? She keeps bringing me gifts and shit. I might take her to a motel and fuck her brains out".

I never had this much attention from women. Each week I was getting jewelry, clothes and all kinds of shit. They all wanted a piece of Jay Bee, smiling at my accomplishments.

I was greeting folks at the door, picking and choosing which women should get into the club. I was standing at the door when this dike named Charlene came into the club, making noise about how she was gonna fuck me up because I was fucking her girl. (The one with the red dress on) Her name was Rosie Funicello from Duck Town in Atlantic City. Anyway, Jimmy Hood stepped to her and convinced her to leave and never come back.

That was the night that I copped her and locked her up. The next few days I put my 7 rules of pimping into play. One week later she was on the track, working for me. (My first Ho)

Keep in mind that I was a shy man coming up. I believed in school and the hard work ethic. I didn't have it so lucky like my friend Cliff. I came from a hard

First Steps into the Game

working middle class family who moved from the country (Salem NJ) to the small suburbs of Atlantic City.

I lived with my mother, father, and siblings on the north side. My father was the first black Bus Driver for The Lincoln Transit Bus Company. My mother was the typical house wife. I had two younger brothers and a baby sister. The city was segregated. The Italians had duck town, the blacks occupied the north side and the whites lived on the South Side of Atlantic Avenue in Ventnor and Margate. Even with the beaches, blacks, whites and Italians and other groups had a section of the beach to themselves.

I never quite fit in with people of my race (Afro-Americans). Some black girls would say that I had too much salt and not enough pepper in my life. I was a book worm, but I wanted to belong with the cool boys, hustlers and boys who sported all the popular women.

I naturally fit in and made friends with Cliff. He and I were alike in a lot of ways. He was white and came from money. He had a car and lived in a big house on the south side of Atlantic City. I hung around whites and felt comfortable and sometimes forgot that I was a black boy. I wanted everything that Cliff had which was money and power.

My family lived in a small row home with six people and three bedrooms. I hated being poor. I often told myself that I was never going to live like my parents. Now, back to my #2 lady! It was about a month later when I met a pretty young white lady by the name of Dorothy. She was a fine 20 year old angel. This blue-eyed beauty from Philadelphia was enough to make a fat man forget about eating chocolate cake. Remember in the Kool and the Gang song "Joanna," the part that goes" Joanna, I love you. You're the one, the one for me"? Man-O-Man Dorothy proves that song right in so many ways.

Even the way we met was like a story out of an Iceberg Slim book (Pimp). You see I was working at the bar that I owned with my main man Cliff, known as the "Chez Paree" (More about the Chez Paree later).

One night while I was working the door, three women walked in. They were from Philadelphia and down in Atlantic City for the weekend. Dorothy was the finest of all three of them. I knew that I had to have her so I put my (7) pimp rules into play.

RULE# 1: THE GOAL
If you want to cop a lady, one thing you need to know is that most women are freakier than you could imagine. They just need a man to bring it out of them. I've heard the way to a man's heart is through his stomach, but the way to a woman's heart (or to what's below it) is through her head. Getting a woman to do anything means making her feel comfortable and secure.

First Steps into the Game

RULE# 2: THE APPROACH
First, you have to be confident. There is nothing like a man with confidence. Say you and you're soon to be lady are going out. You give her a compliment and then you fall back a little bit. Don't over compliment her. Treat her as if you're not tripping off how fine she is. The worst thing you can do is be thirsty. You never want the lady to think you want the pussy more than her. A woman already knows whether or not she's going to give it up, so all you've got to do is not mess up that decision. Don't say anything stupid. Recognize her hotness, but again it's no big deal.

RULE# 3: THE PAGER/PHONE GAME
Make her a little jealous. It's a good thing when you don't ignore your pager/ phone. Don't answer it and be talking in codes but text messages and stuff are cool. You want her to be thinking "Who the hell is he texting?" You want her to want to whip it on you so you won't be texting anyone else. Women are very competitive.

RULE# 4: THE DATE
Take her out somewhere nice and treat it just like a regular date. I like dinner and a movie, but some women like to stay home, some women like walks in the parks, and some women might want to go to the ballet. Wherever you take her, treat her like a lady, open her door, pull out her chair, etc. You can also do really subtle things like touch her leg or rub her shoulders. Try to get really close to let her smell how

good you smell. Don't worry about talking about sex. Remember, you're a pimp.

RULE# 5: IN THE BEDROOM

You have to make her go crazy. Let her know you want it but don't need it. Let her do it to you. Then when you finally get it, take your time. Get familiar with the pussy, it's not going anywhere. It's right there waiting for you to scratch that itch. And don't be selfish and try to hurry up and get yours. That's not pimping. If the lady is going to give you a piece, help her to get hers off first. Now back to the topic at hand.

You want to put yourself as deep as you can inside of her and just let it marinate. Feel around and get familiar with the pussy. Make it jump inside her. Soon she will begin to squirm and beg. You wait until that happens to stroke her, and when you do, begin with slow, deep strokes. She should already be sloppy wet, and throbbing. Then tell her how good her pussy is when you want to make her feel really sexy. The rawer you are, the rawer she will be. Stop making your lady feel like she has to be a Miss Goody-Two-Shoes. Now that's pimping.

RULE# 6: TALK THE TALK

That's another thing; don't be afraid to talk, a woman wants a man who is confident enough to say" pussy." There's nothing better than a man saying how good his lady's "pussy" is. Saying, "This pussy is mine. We can make a fortune with this pussy. That's for real. Like I said, women are freakier than you could ever imagine, but they need to know that they can be a complete slut with you and wake up and you won't think any less of them. Women have an intense physical side that cries out for satisfaction, but one of their biggest fears is that they will be judged. Say "pussy" and talk about how much money she could make with a "pussy" like that. In the heat of the moment whisper it in her ear and it will make her go wild. Yo! It works for me.

RULE# 7 / WALK THE WALK
Don't false advertise. If you don't know what to do with the pussy, then don't act like you know what to do with it. If you have that swagger and you tell her that you are going to tear that pussy up, then you get her in the bedroom and you can't do anything, then you're a trick not a pimp. But if you say to her that you're not that good yet, she will think that she can mold you to be the kind of lover that she likes. Women are like that. Keep Pimping!

After putting my rules into play for about three weeks, she was now on her way to becoming my first turn out. Telling me how much she loved me, bringing me small gifts and calling me every 5 minutes. She was hooked like a crack head. "I knew it was only my doggie style though."

One day around noon, we were chilling at my crib when I decided to lock her down. I asked her, "Do you really love me enough to do anything for me?" She said, "Yeah." So I said, "Even turn a trick?" She said "Anything daddy." So now was the time to school this bitch on the pimp game, like how to turn a trick. For those that don't know it, tricking is not something that a woman knows how to do without some kind of training.

A real pimp will educate his ladies to the do's and don'ts of Trickology. Like the reasons they call a trick a trick is because you're tricking them into thinking that they are getting something that they aren't. (More about trickology later) So after sitting her down and educating her on how the game was going to go down, I got up, put on my clothes and told her that I would be back.

After sliding into my Fleetwood De Elegantz, I started cursing down Atlantic Avenue to check up on my trap from my bottom lady. I received a call on my car phone from Sticks, "an old pool player" to meet him at KY and the curb in front of Timbuktu bar. He was my eyes and ears on the street. He kept me up on what was going on and everything that was creeping or crawling on the streets.

A dude like Sticks is what every player needs on these mean streets. It could be rough especially when you had back stabbing mother fuckers who pretended

First Steps into the Game

to be your friends when all they want is to see you fall on your ass.

While me and my shinny white Caddy was cruising down Atlantic Avenue, I increased my speed and headed to the Timbuktu bar. Sticks was a version of Chris Rock on crack. He stumbled to the car, barely missing the curb. I pressed the button to lower the window. He slurred the words, "Hey Jay Bee, I got some shit for you man. "Can I get in."? "Hell no. Meet me in back of Grace's in five minutes."

I parked the car and walked in back of Grace's to see Sticks. He was leaning on the brick wall for support. "O.K, man spill it, what the fuck's up," I said gettin' down to business. I was not one to make small talk, especially if it was costing' me money.

Sticks laid it out for me about a new pimp from Florida that came to town named Gator. This nigga thought he was the shit and the streets were his, like he could take over any streets in any city he came to. His ho's are so bad they could put you out of business, looking like they came off the cover of Cosmopolitan Magazine. Sticks told me this nigga' was operating without a license. (An Ok Blessing from the Resident Pimp)

"OK man", I reached into my pocket and peeled off a C- Note and thanked him for the 411. "I'll check you later." I'll teach that motherfucker that you don't work in my city without checking in and operating without a license from me.

I headed backed to my parked car, slid behind the wheel and headed towards the track to find this nigga Gator. I spotted him standing in front of the bookstore on Illinois and Pacific Avenue in the middle of the ho stroll.

I parked and got on my car phone and called my man Marlon (Mar-Mar for short). I rapped to him about this pu-butt pimp from Florida, named Gator. I told Mar-Mar it was time to put some work in.

Marlin said, "Word, a favor for a favor?" "Favor for a favor, straight up." I didn't have to say another word. Mar-Mar knew that it would be a handsome pay day for his crew. Jay Bee was a man of his word. When he called, Mar-Mar knew it meant a payday.

While sitting behind my wheel for ten minutes, Mar-Mar and his crew rolled up on Gator on the corner of Arctic and Pacific Avenues. They pulled the dark blue van near the curb. Mar-Mar jumped out and snatched Gator into the Van. One of the men named Tony laid out a serious blow to Gator's jaw. Mar-Mar held the gun to his head while they stripped Gator naked and

First Steps into the Game

tied him up. "So my man, Mar-Mar said, "I hear you some kind of pimp trying to take my man's business.

Well, let me be the first to tell you, it ain't gonna happen! Jay Bee has the streets on lock down, so we gonna take you on a trip out of town.

After Mar-Mar and his crew put in their work, they headed down the Atlantic City Express way. I called my bottom lady to get her ass over to Martin Luther King and Pacific Avenue to pick up the three snow bunnies. They were told that each had three dates at the Rue Rest Hotel. The dates are spending three hundred a piece for white girls, to get a half and half. So off they went in my Lady's car.

On my way to the Rue Rest Hotel, I pulled alongside of my bottom lady's car. Me and my bottom lady pushed the white ho's into the back seat of my car. They were still confused from seeing Gator get snatched into the van and didn't know what was going.

With all of them in my back seat, I parked my car in the Rue Rest Hotel's parking lot and ran it down to the three snow bunnies about their pimp taking a trip and what would happened to them if they didn't jump in line.

I let these bitches know who I was and who this city belonged too. "Your ass is gonna get the same treatment as Gator unless y'all make the right choice tonight." I knew keeping these bitches meant big money in my pockets.

"My choosing fee (fee that a ho pays a pimp to be with him) is $2,500 a piece. I know you don't have $2,500 between the three of you.

I don't care how fine you look, so this is what I'm gonna do. I'll take what you have and put you on a layaway plan until you come up with the rest.

"Now what you gonna do? Shit or get off the pot cause it's real pimpin' going on in Atlantic City."

What can I say! They chose me that night and I had three more snow bunnies on my crew, or so I though.

The next morning, I got a call from Mar-Mar. He laid out what happened last night.

I had told Mar-Mar to take Gator on a little trip out of town. I didn't have to say another word— it was understood. I headed home and waited for my call from Mar-Mar but fell asleep. The next day, I called him and told him to meet me at the Chez Paree in twenty minutes at New York and the board.

When Mar-Mar arrived at the Chez Paree, I spotted him talking to some white bitch at a table. I approached the table and nodded in the white girls' direction and she immediately got up and left.

I patted Mar-Mar's shoulder and as I sat down I said "How's it hanging?" I nodded to Mar-Mar to look down on the floor as I slid a bag towards his foot. "A favor for a favor!" The bag contained a half a key of girl that I had gotten from D-Don. (One of the biggest dealers around)

Marlon shook his head. "Bro, that's why you're my nigga. You one of those nigga's that I'll do anything for cause you a real down nigga, a true pimp.""Can I say something to you man?"

"Run it bro," I said "Ok man. I remember when you and that Italian opened this club. No other nigger

First Steps into the Game

could have pulled off some shit like that and on the south side too."

"But, check this out, man. My game is on the north side and is going strong on Kentucky Avenue," Mar-Mar said. "You're smart as hell and the only nigga I know who can work with the Italians."

Check this out Mar-Mar, "Pimpin is my game, not my name. I pimp Ho's, I pimped yesterday and made it tomorrow. I pimped daylight until she became midnight." Before Mar-Mar made his move to leave, he slapped me a high-five and I walked behind the bar and pulled out the money for him.

"Thanks Jay Bee. Don't hesitant to call on me for anything. I have your back." I took out a bottle of wine and poured two glasses. "Here, this is to us and more money. Now I can take Gator's women and give them a permanent employer." Mar-Mar laughed while holding up his glass to toast with me and left with the bag.

I finished my business with Mar-Mar and was glad I had my streets back. No one is going to step on my toes. Working in this game is a business.

I sat back in my chair and sipped some more wine remembering like it was yesterday.

While I was a student at Atlantic City High, I learned from the guineas about running ho houses when I was an errand boy at the 500 club, thanks to Cliff. The 500 club was the place where all the gangsters and celebrities hung out. You could find Frank Sinatra and Sammy Davis playing at the club. I felt privileged that I was allowed in. There was a race policy, no niggas allowed except those who parked cars or washed the dishes.

That was an opportunity of a life time to manage this club. That was when my life changed. I finished up my business with my prospective client. "Misty, have you decided on what your plans are?" She shrugged her shoulders. "I'm not sure if I want to make a living sleeping with men."

I was losing patience with this woman. I could sense doubt in her voice. "You're so fine. You don't know how much potential you have. You sleep with men anyway, so why not make money too." I took a deep breath, now she was getting on my last nerve but I had to keep pushing. I almost had her in my hands. "I can get you pretty clothes and get your hair done.

I only pick the best women to work for me," I boasted, nothing, but white women!" She batted her long eye lashes and smiled while stepping closer to me. I could smell the sweet scent of roses. I was impressed already. She smelled good and I inspected her nails. Her neatly manicured nails and her make-up were not overly done. Her hair smelled good too.

I had my eye on her the first time she came into my club. She was a stunning beauty with big brown eyes and big tits like the white men loved and she had love silky hair. White men loved that shit and it was easy to get the white women into all kinds of places that black women were banned from. White women were docile. They did what they were told and listened.

Black women had too much mouth. They wanted to tell you how to run things. I didn't need that shit, so I had to go with white women working for me. If I wanted to make money I had to use what the customer liked. "Jay Bee, I thank you for believing in me." I kissed her on the cheek. "Let's give this thing a try." "All right, Jay Bee."

I clapped my hands and smiled. I had another recruit added to my list. Now I had to set the rules straight with this bitch. All my women had to learn the Jay Bee rules before they worked for me.

I had mini boot camps that tested the endurance of the women to stand up to all kinds of shit. Plus, they had to have my choosing fee of $2,500 and pass my test to be in and if they failed, the ho's were history. I had no time for games. I ran my operation like a business. Something I learned from the guineas running their ho houses. I was schooled by the best.

After having a taste, I did not want to go back to being broke. It's something about the smell of green that leaves you with a taste for wanting more. They trusted me to go pick up their money at a ho house on Georgia Ave. That was my first exposure to the business. "Misty, I need you to prove your loyalty to me. I want to give you your first task. You have three days to make one grand. I'll set you up on all locations. The rest should be easy. I can throw in a few clients too."

Now I need you to come over to my business address tomorrow for a three day training session." I handed her a piece of paper with my home address. "I have business to attend to."

I waited at the club for Cliff to come by. I wanted him see the ladies that Gator had left behind. Twenty minute later, Cliff rolled into the Chez Paree. "Hell Jay, I see you're early today. I came by when you called."

"I have a lot on my mind. The business at the club is picking up. I see business is getting good and everybody is making their share of the profits." I nodded my

First Steps into the Game

head and admired the work that we had put in to make this the number one hot spot in Atlantic City.

Cliff, I want you to take a ride with me on Pacific Avenue where I have my girls. There are some new girls in town that I'm thinking about adding to my list," I said taking a sip of wine. We can leave the drop money with Donnie. Remember we have to pay him his money and the other cops too. Everyone has their hands out.

Having the cops on our payroll helped us out. Plus they give me a heads up on when the busts are going to go down. You know how it is when they do their usual round up on the streets. I can get my ho's off the blocks. I ain't had any problems since your old man hooked us up with the cops."

I rolled up to the three women smiling, riding in my shiny Cadillac. " Hello ladies, I'm Jay Bee, remember, the number one pimp on the streets in Atlantic City. I came to inform you that Gator had to take an unexpected trip out of town."

The three women looked at me, with suspension written on their faces. The tall dark haired beauty spoke up. "You lying, Gator would never leave us here alone. He brought us here to work in Atlantic City."

I was beginning to get annoyed with these bitches. "Let me make this clear to you, Gator is not here anymore. You ladies do not have a choice." I smiled. "You can either work for me like I told you last night or take your ass on the first bus or plane out of town," I snapped. "I don't have time for games."

The tall dark haired woman cut her eyes at me. "We want Gator back!" We ain't gonna work for you, hell no." "I see you're the spokes person for the group. You think for everyone?" I said getting out of my car and stepping up to her. "What the hell are you going to do? You have one minute to make up your mind. After that I'm going to take you to the nearest bus station. If you stay you have to work for me."

"I'm going back to Florida. I am not gonna work for you." "You can take your ass back now. What about the rest of you?" The two other women looked at the tall one for an answer. "You're a grown women. You can do what you want. I 'm headed back to Florida." The other women spoke up. "I might stay here. I like this small town." After talking shit. the ladies climbed into the back seat of the car.

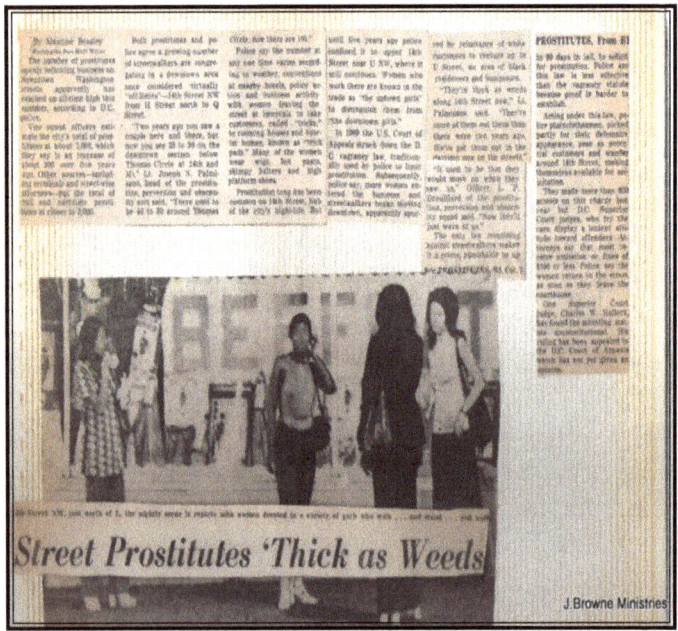

First Steps into the Game

Making the stroll on Pacific Avenue was a good investment that me and my partner, "Wayne" had made. You see, before Pacific Avenue, the women were working on the Boardwalk. Wayne Burton was a good friend and business man who taught me how to expand my business to the stroll on Pacific Avenue and from that day forward, I was making more cash than I could count. The stroll was a gold mine for me.

CHAPTER 3

"IT'S ALL ABOUT THE MONEY. THE MONEY GETS THE HONEY"

l-r Jimmy Olive, disc jockey, J.B., the man with master plan, Erik Davenport, bouncer, Dee Shute, assistant manager, Pete Vantol, porter, Don Ransome, 2nd bar-

"It's all about the money. The money gets the honey"

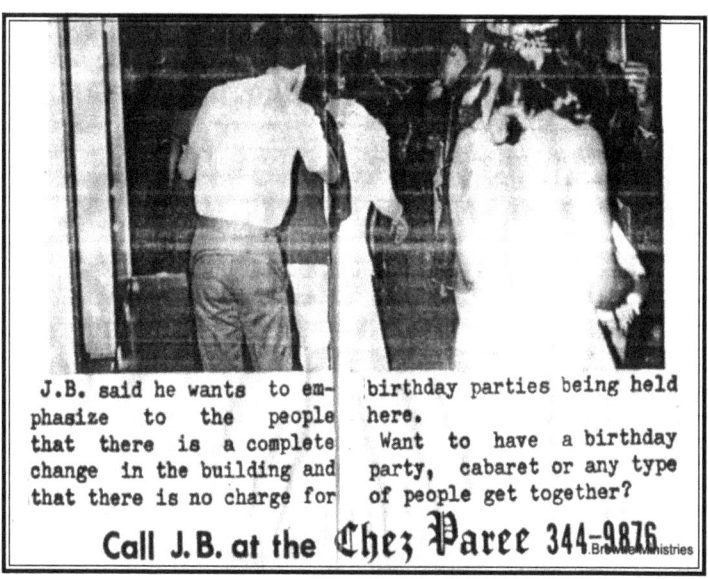

The Club was popping all night. I was making money from ho's and the club. Cliff and I had more cash than we could spend. I was at the bar looking for potential recruits. My business mind never slept. I was always thinking about making money. I saw Dorothy sitting at the bar as I was making my rounds checking things out in the club. I gave her a smile and walked up to her. "Hey Baby," I said stroking her hair gently. She gazed at me with a happy look on her face.

She inspected me from top to bottom. I took her hand and spun her around. She opened up her purse and pulled out a small box. "This is for you, Jay. I wanted to show you that I really love you."

I took the box and put it in my pocket. A big Italian dude came and stood next to me while grabbing Dorothy by the hand (He was the trick that she had drive her to the bar). She tried to pull away and I said, "I don't think she wants to go with you!" and called my man Jimmy Hood over to talk to this guy. After Jimmy had talked to him he came to me and Dorothy and apologized over and over until Jimmy had to come over and escort him out of the club.

I took Dorothy across the street to a neighborhood hotel. The two story hotel was easy access for couples to get their grove on. The rooms were modestly priced. The receptionist was a middle aged white woman over 190 pounds. She was use to the crowd coming and going for one or two nights. She never saw the same couple twice. Sometimes folks used fake names and driver's license.

This was a hotel that didn't care about the correct information. She looked at me and at this white woman on my arm. She turned up her lip and shook her head in disgust. After I paid her for the room, she threw the keys on the counter and I snatched them up. Dorothy could barely hold herself up. I held her by the arm trying to make sure that she did not fall.

I unlocked the door number 256. The room was dark with a mildew scent. I held my breath while I tried to hold Dorothy by her left arm. The hotel did not leave room for decorations. There was a king size bed and an end table near the bed and a mid size dresser. The room was suited for one purpose. It was not a honeymooner's first choice.

I laid this Italian woman on the bed and helped her undress. She giggled and lifted her head several times to kiss me. I marveled at the sight of her body. Never had I seen such a work of art. I got an instant hard on.

"It's all about the money. The money gets the honey"

Man-o-man, I had to use all my business savvy and remembered what I had come to the hotel for. I took off my shirt and lay down on top of Dorothy. "Come on daddy, I want to see your big black dick. I hear all black men are packing," she said kissing my nipples. I immediately jumped to my knees looking down at her. "What's wrong, did I do something wrong, please tell me, so I can fix it," she pleaded over and over.

I sat on the edge of the bed sulking. "My rent is overdue. I'm a month behind and I might get put out on the street tomorrow." She started kissing my back, trying to ease my mind. "How much you need. You know I'll do anything for you." "Five hundred," I said, keeping my head low.

As she was getting off the bed she said "I have some money on me. Take it", she said going into her purse. No daddy of mine is going to be on the streets."

I took the money and put it in my pants pocket. I was full of confidence and life. I was a hot commodity in Atlantic City with all the right ingredients; young, handsome, single and the manager of one the hottest night clubs.

I had ho's bringing me gifts and shit. The business side of me was talking to me as Dorothy began rubbing her body on me. I climbed on top of her stroking her real good. She moaned and moaned until she came twice. I came shortly after and lifted myself off of her breathing hard.

She lay there with a smile plastered on her face. "This was the best I had in a long time. I swear you can make a woman do anything the way you stroke it." The business side of me took over as I lay there thinking about my plans for Dorothy. I wanted to know how far she would go for me.

I cut my business short for now with Dorothy and headed back to the club. I didn't have time to lay up with this bitch. It was business. I had proved to myself that she would do anything for me.

I walked into the club conducting business as usual that night. I fought my way into the crowded club. Jimmy stood by the door checking ID's and turning the undesirables away. This was my favorite part of the night.

There was this one dude who was thrown out of the club but he refused to go away. He started shouting and waving his fist in the air. "Shit man, I ain't do a damn thing, that woman was asking of it all night. She teased me and I wanted more. Shit, women shouldn't tease a man and make his dick hard".

"I want to come back in" he shouted. Jimmy stepped to the tall man. He was a big man about the same size as Jimmy. Jimmy did not hesitant to take on any man. He grabbed the white man by the collar and threw him against the wall. The man looked at this black bouncer in awe like a black man should not grab a white man and if he does, he has consequences to face.

"That's why I was slow to let niggas, white or black in the club. I try to give them a chance and they fuck it up for everyone," I said shaking my head. Jimmy took out his .38 and hit the man across the right side of his face. I watched the blood trickle down his cheek and into his mouth.

I felt an adrenaline rush take over. I felt a surge of power and accomplishment of getting money from

"It's all about the money. The money gets the honey"

another prospect, Dorothy. I felt like I was on top of my game now that things were falling into place: money, women, clothes, power and the club.

Jimmy and I walked back into the crowded club with the music vibrating off the walls. There were straight and gay couples dancing on the floor. Jimmy returned back to his post, manning the front door for any more trouble.

I went to the back office to get a quick breather from the crowd. I stretched out on the sofa and was in a dream state thinking about what took place in the motel room with Dorothy. I could not believe that a white woman would hand over $600 with just a word. It was too easy.

I thought about all the gifts I had accumulated since me and my partner took over as managers for the Chez Paree. It was like a dream. I was nineteen years old and living like a king. My partner came in shortly, barging through the door. I was awakened from my dream of living large. "Yo! Jay Bee, how did things go down with that girl?" Cliff winked. I know you must've hit it hard."

"She gave up the money. It was too easy. I told her that I was behind on my rent and the landlord was ready to evict me to the streets. She gave me six hundred dollars with no problem. I just wondered how many women I can get to give me that kind of money."

"Shit, if it's that easy, I can get a string of women to give me money," I said smiling while lounging on the sofa. "Those Italians are running a ho house on Georgia Avenue. I can get some of those fellas to give me a quick lesson on running ho's as a business."

Cliff sat at the desk. "Jay, you're always thinking about making money. Do you ever think about anything else?"

I laughed out loud, "Yeah! Pussy and money. There is nothing else. I wanna make it big in this world. I ain't gonna go to no damn college for four years to come out and make peanuts. Look at us Cliff, we are young and making a good living managing this club. We're getting popular around town. I had offers to go to the Club Harlem as a guest next week. Everything is on the house. I say we venture down there and mingle with our folks."

The following evening I showered, allowing the warm water to pour all over my body. I stood motionless in the shower soaking up the warmth from the warm water. I went into my room and picked out a tan suit that was hanging in the walk-in closet as I looked in the mirror and admired my curly hair.

You see I was lucky to have a light complexion. This way I had more of an advantage than the dark skinned brothers in the city. I used all my assets to my advantage.

I was accepted into most places of my peers because of my color. I hated the color line that divided the blacks in the city but that was the way it was. I just became numb to the color issues in the city. The racial injustices continued to grow and the restlessness of the people was coming to a head with the militant organizations like the Black Panthers. They were a group that fought for justice for blacks at all levels. Most people feared them, but they were actually warm hearted black men fighting for a cause. I dressed in

"It's all about the money. The money gets the honey"

one of my best suits for this evening. I slipped on a pair of tan slacks and a black silk shirt with matching shoes and I waited for my partner to pick me up.

Fifteen minutes and a horn began blowing outside my town house. We only had a few blocks to go to the club. "My man, what's up?" "I'm thinking about getting it on with this honey at the club, she's a blonde with the big tits. I like big tits on a woman," Cliff laughed. "I know what you mean, "I said chiming in while pulling the mirror down to inspect myself. "Damn I'm one fine nigga."

"You're too conceited. I think these ho's are filling your head with too much shit." We both laughed as we turned right on New York Avenue on the way to the Chez Paree. Cliff had a sly grin on his face. "Maybe you can get her to put in some work for you."

"Work," I said looking confused. "What kind of work?" Cliff looked me like I was stupid. "Making these women make some real money trickin'. Look, they already love you and they give you gifts. Look how easy it is now. Just think about all the money you could make," Cliff said proudly.

When Cliff and I arrived at the Chez Paree on New York Avenue, there was a small line assembling outside the door. The street was the center of the night life besides Kentucky Avenue. Before entering the building, I zeroed in on Dorothy standing first in line.

She had a box in her right hand. "Hello, Daddy", she called grinning. "I have something special for you." I looked at this luscious, dark Italian beauty. "Come," I said grabbing her arm. "You're my special guest for tonight." There were other women behind Dorothy trying to bid for my attention. I looked at all my potential clients and hoped that I could somehow use these women to make money and more money.

I kissed Dorothy on the lips gently, running my hands down her silky hair. She smiled and turned the color of crimson. I took the package and walked towards the back office. I knew that she would be working for me later tonight.

Shortly before 1:00am, the club was packed with party goers from straight to gays. There was a steady crowd going and coming. I knew this was going to be a long night. Most people who came to party stayed until the rising of the sun.

Later that night I found Dorothy hanging around the bar talking to Silk the bartender most of the night. Then I spotted her sitting alone at the bar. I made my way fighting the crowd to get to her.

Mad as hell, I put on my pimp charm. "Hello, I'm looking for the most beautiful woman here tonight. Someone told me she was sitting here," I said smiling. She turned red and stared into my eyes. I planted a kiss on her lips. I said, "Baby it's time to get to work," and she said "Okay daddy," and got up and went to the bar to talk to some trick that had been checking her out all night. Well, my thoughts were, I have her now! The rest should be easy.

Now that the club was taking care of itself, I decided to take my ladies on a working road trip to New York. The three that went to New York were the three that I got from Gator. Well, one of the first things that I learned was never put all your girls down in

"It's all about the money. The money gets the honey"

one place together. That's when they start plotting on your ass.

Anyway these ladies gave me more hell over that weekend then I've had in my whole "Pimp Career". I think my trap for the whole weekend was about $1,500 from all three of them and I had to spend most of that on hotel rooms. Every time that I went to check on their traps, they were all huddled up under each other. Now this was around June or July on Avenues of America about 8:00 pm. Tricks were all over the place and no police. What the fuck?

I parked my car and got out, walked up to them and got all up in their shit about getting my money, split them up and got back in my car. This went on all weekend, until Sunday night when I picked them up to leave New York.

I was riding nice and high from doing a one-on-one (snorting cocaine) and drinking some root beer soda coming down the Atlantic City Express Way on my way from New York City with two of my ho's in the back seat and one in the front.

I was mad as hell because they didn't make the kind of money that I had longed for. This was a fucked up weekend for me with my stash going low. I was not in the mood for bullshit. I almost hit a road sign along the expressway when I heard laughter coming from the back seat of my white Cadillac. "What the hell is so funny I yelled?" I turned my head around and gave my "don't fuck with me look".

"Nothing Jay Bee, Silvia spoke up. She was the leader for the pack. She could hold her own but this time I was getting angry as hell. I said, "What the hell is so funny?" I asked a second time. Bunny in the front seat started her giggling again.

I pulled my car over on the side of the road. "I ain't having no back talk. Now you bitches want an ass kicking then that's what I'm gonna do," I said getting out the car. I ordered everyone out of the car. "Now take off your damn clothes. All the women had stopped their laughter. Now everyone feared the worse.

The women started shivering and holding their hands over their chest. "I see no one has a damn thing to say," I walked up to each one and slapped each one across the face. There was silence. Sylvia, the spokes person did not bite her tongue. "We did nothing wrong, but laugh," she protested.

I walked up to Sylvia, giving her another slap on the face so hard she went down on the ground. I proceeded to kick her in the ribs. No ho is going to talk back unless I give them permission and I found myself slowly transforming into something I was not quite aware of. I couldn't put my finger on it, but I felt like a new man at 20 years old.

Now I was riding high with all the women up my ass. I was getting more gifts and money from these women coming into the club trying to score. I never had this much pussy thrown in my face. It's like picking cherries.

Three days later after the New York trip, I had got a call from a pimp name Danny Row from Boston. He was calling to serve me the news that all three girls had chose him.

"It's all about the money. The money gets the honey"

JAY! JAY! JAY BEE! Jay Bee wake-up! Wake-up, dinner's ready. "Wow" what a dream. Dale had just awakened me from one hell of a dream. As I went to wash up for dinner I was thinking about telling Dale about my dream. So as I sat down to eat, I decided to tell her after we said grace. As I was telling her, she stopped me and said "I was part of all that, don't you remember? You men never get the story right. The one thing that you forgot was when we met. Let me lay the story out for you."

CHAPTED 4

DALE TELLS THE REAL DEAL ON HOW THEY MET.

First of all we met during the autumn of 1972. My sister Linda began going to a club in Atlantic City called the "Chez Paree" which was located on New York Avenue at the Boardwalk. This is where we met, if you don't remember. You were really into clothes (fashions) and loved to have them designed for you. Linda told me that you always complimented her on

Dale tells the real deal on how they met.

her outfits and asked where she got them from? She told you that her mom and her sister made them for her. You then said, "Why don't you bring them to the club to meet me. I'm interested in having some clothes made for me?"

So, in September, Linda brought me and mom to the "Chez Paree" to meet you. We walked in and there you stood, a six foot tall man with a pretty medium brown complexion and brown eyes, shoulder length hair, mustache, a very pretty smile **AND** a 29-inch waist. You were the type of man that a woman would like right away. At that time you were twenty-five years old and when asked, would not admit whether or not you were married, so in my nineteen year old mind, it did not matter. Later, I found out that you lived with someone and you were married (although separated).

I thought to myself, now here is a man who at our first meeting, seemed like a dream come true. You seemed to be the kind of person who would really listen to what a woman had to say, put that person at ease and make her laugh.

After spending a few hours talking and getting to know you, mom and I took your measurements and made notes on the kinds of clothes you wanted us to make for you. Then you invited us all to come back the next weekend for a special event that you were having at the "Chez Paree." Linda and I returned for the event and had a ball.

As I look back on how things went, I do not remember you asking me to come back after. It's like we just fell into some kind of routine – one that we both accepted. It's as if we both knew that we were meant to be together without either one of us saying a word. (At least, that's how it was in my mind.) Your friends at the club knew that I was "Jay Bee's woman!"

Your job at the club (or so you told me) was a little bit of everything – electrician, bouncer, DJ – you name it, you did it and was good at it. Never once did you say that you were part owner with your friend. At that time, you were a very private person, only telling people what you wanted them to know. You were well liked at the club and seemed to know just about everyone.

The club was patronized mostly by the gay population although a lot of straight people found their way there and you started telling me about who was gay or straight, who was going through a sex change operation and at what stage they were at or if they were taking hormone shots or pills. Everyone loved to talk to you and tell you all of their business.

Most weekends, I could be found in Atlantic City with you at the club, and my mom hated that. (The thought of her daughters going to a gay club just did not sit right with her. If you remember, Linda never told mom anything about the club so she did not know about the gay cliental until we came for your measurements and she wasn't happy about it.)

Linda had her own friends that she visited and once getting there, we went our separate ways but usually arrived and left together. Your club was opened from 7:00 pm to 6:00 am but you usually found time to take me to other clubs such as "Dirty Edna's" or out somewhere to eat.

Dale tells the real deal on how they met.

One night, you finally admitted to me that you lived with someone. You also said, "She's white with long blond hair and stands six feet one inch in her stocking feet." I said, "You sure do like them tall. I'm only five feet two inches tall." All you did was laugh and say, "I like how we fit together."

Do you remember the building that you lived in near the old bus station and your neighbor Jerry? Remember when he invited Linda, George Hayes and I to come stay for the weekend with one single bed in his room? He met us at the bus station and took us to his room where we sat talking while waiting for time to get dressed to go to the club. While talking, we heard footsteps in the hall and watched as you came around the corner. Boy, were you surprised! Jerry had never said one word to you about me coming and the look on your face told it all. You nodded at us and continued on into your room and closed the door.

Shortly after you came in, we started getting ready to go to the club. There was only the one little mirror in the bathroom and we had to take turns using it. I remember that while I was putting my make-up on, you came in the bathroom to use the mirror also. The whole time that you were trying to tie your tie, you kept looking at me, not your tie. Finally, you were done and went back to your room, gathered your things and got ready to leave. You stood at the door and asked if we were ready to leave but the whole time you were looking at me. We all said no, so you left but it was clear that you were angry.

We arrived at the club later and I went upstairs to let you know that I was there. The club had two stories, the bar was downstairs and the disco was upstairs where you were the DJ. You walked me downstairs and at the bottom of the steps, you grabbed me by my coat collar and pushed me up against the wall and said, "I'm not jealous, like hell I'm not jealous. It's just that the woman that I love was in the room of a man who isn't even a real man," meaning that Jerry was gay.

We all had a good time hanging out that night and left together to go back to the rooms. Linda, George and Jerry went to his room. You and I went to your room to rest and started watching cartoons.

Finally, we got ourselves together and put our clothes back on. Before I could leave to go back to Jerry's room, we heard a key in the lock. This was my first glimpse of Jennifer. You introduced us and told her that I was a friend of yours who was visiting Jerry with my sister and brother. (Linda and George)

Dale tells the real deal on how they met.

That was my cue to go back across the hall. Linda and George were asleep but Jerry sat up when I opened the door. He took one look at me and said, "That's Jennifer but don't worry, you wore him out. She won't get any now." Even though I knew there was someone else, I was still hurt and angry. I wanted you all for myself but there was something about you that made me forget about being angry at you.

Our relationship progressed with me coming to Atlantic City as often as I could and whatever you wanted, I did. After we had been seeing each other for about seven months, (around Easter of 1973) we were getting something to eat one night and you said, "I was supposed to spend the day with my son, James." That was also when you told me that you were married but that the two of you were separated and had been for a while. Another hurt to get over, but I couldn't get angry since I had never asked you any questions and the information wasn't volunteered. Could I?

One night, while we were in the bar and this crazy looking little lady kept coming and going and each time she would whisper something in your ear. Then she would leave and come back later and do it all over again. This went on for a while so I made my way over to you and sat down to see if I could hear anything.

Sure enough, she came back and I heard you call her Dolly. She said something about money, cops and tricks. Your reply was so low that I couldn't hear it and then Dolly left again. It wasn't until later that evening that I put things together and realized that "YOU WERE A PIMP!"

All that I knew about pimps came from television but I had heard enough to understand what was going on. Well, you certainly did not seem like those guys that I had seen on television. No flashy clothes or big heeled shoes, no jewelry and no flashy car. This made you all the more interesting. Man-oh-man, I couldn't wait to see what happened next and the more I was around you, the more that I found out.

Do you remember how I met Ivy? This one night while we were at the club, she was there and kept looking at me. Finally, she asked you, "Is she your lady?" And you replied, "Yeah, she's mine." Then she said, "Let me know when you're finished with her!" You just smiled and as she walked away, you told me that she was a "Female Pimp." I got angry and said to you, "When you're finished with me, let me know first". One funny moment in our early relationship that I will always remember was around the time that the movie "The Exorcist" came out. It was you, me, Bernard and some of your friends sitting around talking about 6:00 am after the bar had closed. One minute we're all laughing and talking about the movie and the next minute the closet door swung open by itself. Five seconds later, the bar was empty. No one

Dale tells the real deal on how they met.

---

asked any questions, we just looked at each other and took off running.

We had a lot of good times when I came to visit and I usually stayed overnight. We spent most of our time at the bar and that was fine just as long as I could be with you. Our sex life was great. No matter how tired you were after working all night you still took the time to see that I was satisfied.

On this particular Saturday night when I came to Atlantic City to visit you, there was a different female who kept coming in to see you and the two of you would go out into the entrance way hall and you would return alone. Remember? Once she even came in and you could not leave and I saw her slip you some money. I really didn't pay it too much attention since I already knew what you did but a few weeks later, I found out that she worked for you and her name was Dorothy.

Shortly after this, I started having problems at home. Mom wasn't happy about my coming to see you especially at the bar. Then one night when Linda, George and I came down, someone had loosened the lugs on Linda's tires and we had to drive back to Vineland going ten miles an hour. There was also your favorite event – the night that Linda's car got stolen and my mom and dad came to get us. Dad was pissed. I remember you going outside to talk to him and promised that you would bring me home in the morning after the bar closed.

Little did I know that these events and the problems I was having at home were some of the deciding factors that made you ask me to move to Atlantic City. You made me feel wanted and I always hated when it was time to go home, so when you asked me about moving, I gladly said yes. I remember the room that you got for me at the Summit Motel and then told me that Dorothy had a room down the hall. She and I got to spend a lot of time together and I realized that I actually liked her.

We had our good times and our bad times and once during our bad times in December of 1974, I left and went back home to Vineland. I had left the two of you together because I felt that your way of life was not for me. I called my mom and she came to get me. Guess she would do anything to get me away from you. I was so scared that you would come after me that I felt that I could not stay at home so I went over to my ex-boyfriends apartment and stayed for a few days. His name was Harold Lewis.

Dale tells the real deal on how they met.

After I returned to mom's house, I settled into a daily routine of looking for work and helping to keep the house clean. Then, one night you called me. I remember it clearly. It was February 15, 1975 and mom answered the phone and told me that I had a call. When I picked up the receiver, this male voice says, "Happy Valentine's Day." I asked, "What did you say?" And to this you replied, "Happy Valentine's Day, even if it is a day late." My reply was, "Thank you! Now who is this?" and when you said, "Jay Bee," I dropped the phone. We talked for a few minutes and then you said that you wanted us to get back together, I told you that I would like that but that we would have to get together and talk about it before making any decisions. You asked me if I was pregnant and I said yes. Then you asked me if it was yours and I told you that I honestly did not know.

So, you decided to come to Vineland that night so we could talk and naturally mom did not want me to go anywhere with you. The end result of our talk was that we got back together, in a way. We decided that I would stay at mom's house and that you would come visit me when you could. I was the square girl in your life so I stayed away from your business as much as possible. Most of the time that we spent together we had to sneak around to be with each other because mom still didn't like you. Remember? Did we care? Hell no!!

The summer of 1975 sped by with you visiting me quite often and on September 13th, I gave birth to a son. Hell, I wasn't prepared for a boy. I only had a girl's name picked out. It was my cousin Frankie who came up with the name Marquis' and I picked the middle name of Adrien. So he was named Marquis' Adrien Evans.

You were out of town and did not know that the baby was born until a week later, but you were happy about it. Marquis' was about two months old before you finally got a chance to see him. You called me and wanted me to come and spend the weekend with you at your apartment. The only problem was that your car was in the shop so you had us to catch a cab from Vineland to Pleasantville which you happily paid for.

We had a nice time together and your parents even showed up. Marquis' was in the bedroom and when your mom found out there was a baby in the house, she made her way in there to see him. She took one look at him and said, "He looks just like Jimmy did when he was a baby."

Later that evening you got a call and had to fly out to Kentucky. You told me that I didn't have to leave until the next day, left me cab fare and some spending money. You also said to make sure that I didn't forget anything. Evidently, you didn't want Dorothy to know that we had been there.

A few months later, you had Marquis' and I move back to Atlantic City and back into the Summit Motel again. I ended up applying for county assistance so that I could take care of Marquis'. This is when you went with Cliff to Allentown, Pennsylvania to help work on the bar that you guys were building up there.

During one of your trips home, you found a two bedroom upstairs apartment for us. By this time, I was pregnant again. We had talked about terminating the

Dale tells the real deal on how they met.

pregnancy and decided against it, so we moved into the apartment as planned. This was the first place that I had seen in a long time that still had radiators. The only flaw with them was that they leaked and there were mushrooms growing out of the rub where the water fell. Later on, we found out that the place also had mice that only came out at night. Marquis' was free to play and walk around during the daytime but nighttime we were either on the couch or in the bed with the covers tucked under the mattress. We kept the apartment for several months. This is where Marquis' started to walk, learned to talk and was potty trained.

On August 19, 1977, our daughter LaQuenta Nichole Evans was born and as usual, you were nowhere to be found. I walked a block to use the pay phone to call and let your mom and Bonnie know where I was and made arrangements for my friend Sandy to come and get Marquis' from the neighbors house and take him to my mom's. I carried my suitcase downstairs and outside myself and went to the hospital. LaQuenta was born between 11:00 am and 12:00 noon but you didn't show up until the following morning, walking in like you had only gone for coffee. Boy was I pissed.

You never asked how I was, if it was a difficult birth or if either of our lives had been in danger and I felt as if you didn't care. You came in with three roses and a big grin on your face and if I had a gun, I would gladly have shot you. The day I was to come home, you borrowed a car and came to pick me up. You had three red roses and wanted to hold the baby and ride in the wheelchair and got a little miffed because the nurse said no.

On the way home, we stopped by your mom's house to show her the baby but only Bonnie was home and got to see her. Then we proceeded on home. You would have thought that I had been gone for weeks instead of three days. There were dirty dishes in the sink and all over the counter In Marquis' room, you had clothes all over the bed because you couldn't decide what to wear and didn't bother to hang them back up.

In the bathroom, the tub and sink needed to be cleaned, but what hurt the most was our bedroom. I had put clean sheets on the bed before going to the hospital because my water had started leaking. These sheets had blood stains on them which meant that you were screwing someone in our bed while I was in the hospital. And this is the man who says, "I LOVE YOU!" The bad part was that I had to clean the apartment, get dressed to go to the drugstore for pads and passed your mom's house.

When I arrived at your mom's house, she asked me, "didn't you just get out of the hospital?" To which I replied, "Yes!" She then asked, "Why aren't you home in the bed?" and I said, "Because your son told me that if I needed something from the store, I had better get dressed and go get it and to stop past her house and tell Bonnie to bring him the bike." Your mom told me to go home and tell "JIMMY" to come see her when you leave the house. I did just that and from the look on your face, you dreaded going over there. Never did find out what she said to you.

It was during my hospital stay that you got another girl whose name was Rebecca Webber, Becky for short. You told me that you were going to have to spend some

Dale tells the real deal on how they met.

time with her to get her on the right track, or words to that effect. Knowing what you did and accepting it were two different things. Being hurt is another. If you had never her into our home, it wouldn't have been a problem for me. I kept wishing that you would quit and we could get married and settle down to raise the kids. I felt that it wouldn't be fair of me to ask you to quit since I was aware of what you did when we met. But I could wish.

When you tell someone you love them it means that you accept them for who they are, faults and all. So I knew that I had to let you change in your own time because demanding it would only cause resentment later on.

You were spending more and more time between the Chez Paree, the bar in Allentown and your girls that when you were home (during the day) you mostly slept. I tried to keep the kids on a schedule where they slept when you did. This worked for a while and lasted for a few months. Things weren't working out and I was unhappy so we decided that I should move back to Vineland with my mom. I was beginning to resent all of the time that you were spending away from us. The kids and I moved back to Vineland and I got a job while you went about your business and made me feel as if you just didn't care.

After getting settled at moms, I got a job at Kimble Glass (Owens Illinois) which was right across the street from the house. You would come and visit as often as you could and usually brought gifts for the kids. From the end of 1977 until 1983, this was our routine. You visited when you could. I worked and took care of the kids. My babysitters were in the neighborhood, so we didn't have far to go.

Finally it was time for Marquis' to start school and he enjoyed it. Playing with the other kids was just fine with him. And then the time came for Noodle to start school. It just seemed like time was flying by. Christmas was always great and putting those toys together for the kids was rough but fun. I understood how my parents felt when they had to do it.

Marquis' and LaQuenta got used to you not being there and were glad to see you when you finally did show up. It bothered me that you would not stop what you were doing so that we could be together but I believed that if I brought up the subject, it would just make you leave for good.

Do you remember the night when you came to mom's house and no one heard you ring the doorbell? You climbed up on the roof on the back of the house by my room. Usually mom would hear you and answer the door so she suggested that I give you a key so that you would not wake her up. After that, you did better about getting to the house before it got too late.

In 1982, both mom and Linda moved out to California to work for mom's sister Willa Brokenbough. Mom was to work for Willa on Edwards Air Base at her restaurant called the Shawn Dee which was the only civilian business on the base. Linda was to work with Willa's catering company which she ran out of the Chester Washington Gold Course in Los Angeles. When they left, I took over the house which had four bedrooms, two bathrooms, a large living room and dining room with a full attic and full basement. We

Dale tells the real deal on how they met.

also had a huge yard surrounded by hedges with a garage, a pear tree, cherry tree and grape vines in the backyard. This was the house that I grew up in.

The bills were becoming too much for me to handle alone and I ended up renting out two of the bedrooms while keeping one for myself and one for the kids. One room was rented to Alonzo Fuller who was a friend of my brothers and the other to Prudence Ware who was a friend of mine and who also worked at Kimble Glass.

Pru was cool and never gave me any problems and paid her rent on time. Her family was usually in and out but it was no problem, we all got along. She ended up getting pregnant and then her boyfriend Thomas was there a lot so I made sure to either be dressed or have on my robe when I left the room. Also, there was Alonzo to consider. Finally, Pru gave birth to a baby girl who she named Ja' Nee. Pru was the type of person who liked to go out on the weekends but having the baby settled her down.

My problem was Alonzo who did not want to pay his rent. It was always a promise of next week which never came. Finally, I had to put him out and got another tenant named Wayne who was also a friend. His girlfriend was Tammy, who went to school with my sister Linda.

Things got to a point where I could not afford to heat the house and the bills were piling up, so Pru was going to move in with Thomas and I called my mom to get some advice and she said to start making arrangements to come out to California. When I told you about the move, the only thing you said was, "Just don't give me any problems with visiting my daughter." I told you that "she has nothing to do with what was right or wrong between us and as long as she wants to see you, I won't come between the two of you."

CHAPTER 5

"I HAD TO STOP HER"

Okay!, ok, slow your roll sweetheart, you sound like you're trying to retrace your roots or something. Most of what you were saying I remember, but all that other stuff, I think you need Jesus. If you're finished in here let's move into the living room.

Now the kind of things that I was talking about "Miss Dale" was like the time Parker and Poppy busted me with Charlene, Poppy's ho, at my Deer Hollow Woods Apartment where I was living with Dorothy.

Dorothy had convinced Charlene to come home with her after work had been put in. You see Poppy and Charlene were having some problems and as always these girls were always running their mouths talking about stuff that has nothing to do with putting in work.

You have to understand, the pimps that I was hanging out with were all seasoned pimps. We did everything together like car caravanning across the country, taking over the ho-strolls where ever we went, going out to eat together and going horseback riding. We were tight as hell.

So the morning that I came home and saw Charlene in my living room really messed me up. My mind was telling me that I had another lady, one that made good money, but how was I going to tell my friend Poppy that his bottom lady had chose me? You see, this pimp was in love this girl.

As I shook all that square stuff out of my head, I sat down and started to rap to her about being in another pimp's home without choosing. She said that she knows how the game is played and was cool with it. So after she gave me the money, I told her not to leave the apartment until I come back. Dorothy took her to the bedroom so that they could talk and do whatever girls do.

As I was leaving the apartment going to my car, who do you think was parked next to my car? None other than Parker and Poppy! Damn! I wasn't ready to serve this fool yet. I played it cool and just said "what the hell y'all doing here?" Poppy said he was looking for Charlene and wanted to know if Dorothy had seen her. I said that I would ask her when I got back and that I would call him and let him know. I'm thinking that if they saw me leave then they would leave too, so I left.

Little did I know that Parker's girl had seen Dorothy and Charlene catch a cab together from the stroll and told Poppy that she was probably at my apartment and if she was there, then she was choosing.

From Pimpin to the Pulpit

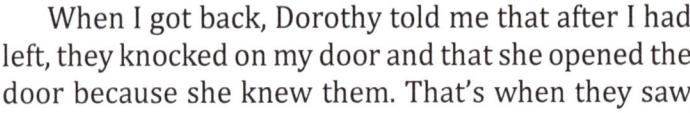

When I got back, Dorothy told me that after I had left, they knocked on my door and that she opened the door because she knew them. That's when they saw

"I Had To Stop Her"

Charlene standing in the background. Poppy told her to get the fuck in his car and told Dorothy to tell me that he would see me later.

Well, later came that night. We were all at the "Hickory House Bar" and I was talking with the "Ragsdale Brothers" (they were the stick-up boys) about a stick-up that happen at the Rue-Rest Hotel the night before. They had robbed the hotel, the tricks and ho's both. Anyway, my lady Becky was one of the ladies in the hotel when it got robed. She knew that it was Kevin Ragsdale and told me after it had happen. After rapping with them for a while, Kevin made a call and we left for their house. Once there, we went to the bedroom where Kevin pulled a bag from under the bed and dumped it on the bed.

Kevin said to me, "Jay, pick out your stuff, we had to take everything from everybody to make it look good. We knew that it was your lady but we couldn't do anything about it at that time". I took my stuff plus Parker and Poppy's stuff. When I got back to the "Hickory House," Parker and Poppy was still there. So I went over to them and put their stuff on the bar top without saying a word. Nothing was ever said about why Charlene was at my house. I think Charlene was trying to play Poppy and make him jealous because she loved him too. Every time that he got a new girl, she would run her off. I had made $1,500 from the whole thing plus it let everybody know that pimping was going on in my house.

Damn! Baby, can you believe after all this time, I can still remember damn near all that went on back in the day? Even after you and the kids went to California and Becky (Rose) was my bottom lady. There was this time when I had just copped these too new ladies from a Boston pimp name Foots.

I had just pulled up to my man Honey B's house in Boston. I was there to kick it with him and see if I could get chosen. His lady Patty was about to leave for the stroll as I was walking into the house and over heard me telling Honey that I needed to be chose this week end.

Later after we got dressed for the stroll, Honey was telling me about a night that these two "Twin Midget Pimps" from Detroit had come to town riding in a red and gold limo calling them self's "Ali-Baba and the Forty Thieves" because they had about 40 ho's between them. The cops closed the stroll down because them ho's were stealing and ripping off every trick in town and the stroll had just opened back up so the pimping was back on.

I was in luck. We walked the stroll and ended up in one of the clubs that ho's and tricks hung out at. As I was having a drink I saw this fine girl walk into the bar looking like a celebrity who's trying to attract and avoid the paparazzi at the same time. She was model thin, wearing a hat, jeans, and a T-shirt that says "Bitch" we made eye contact and I knew that before the night was over I was going to have this lady.

Patty had just come into the club and as Honey was about to go over to her and check his trap, I asked him to ask Patty who was the girl with the hat on. When he came back he said that her name was Paris and she was with a pimp name Foots.

"I Had To Stop Her"

Now Foots was a crazy freaked out pimp that looked like a 6ft 4in black gorilla. The word was he got his name from breaking his foot of in ho's ass. He was one bad ass nigger that no one wanted to fuck with. That's why nobody messed with his girls and that's why they acted like they were the shit.

Anyway, after putting in a whole night of trying to "cop a ho", me and Honey went back to his crib. Honey and I were in the kitchen for about an hour or so when Patty came home and came into the kitchen and said "Guess what daddy? I have a surprise for Jay Bee." We both looked at her like what the hell you talking about. Before we could say anything, she called for Paris and her wife-in-law to come into the kitchen. Patty said that they wanted to choose me but we would have to leave that night.

Well you know that I had no problem with that. I collected my choosing money and we said our good-byes and left. Once in the car and heading for Atlantic City, I asked the girls to tell me something about themselves. That's when they told me about Foots. How they had no way to get away from him because everybody was scared of him and that they was so grateful that I allowed them to chose me that they would do whatever I wanted them to do.

After working them in Atlantic City for about 2 days, my boys and I decided to take a road trip. We all car caravanned to Florida while stopping at the truck stops on the way to put in work.

Once we arrived in Florida and got our motel rooms, we took a trip to the stroll and showed the girls where they would be working. Everything went very well for about 2 weeks. Then things got slow, so we decided to take our show over to New Orleans.

"I Had To Stop Her"

Little did I know that this was going to be my biggest test as of yet. New Orleans was jumping. Pimps from all over the country were there. The strip joints were jumping. Tricks were all over the streets 24-7 action. I called Becky back in Atlantic City and told her where we were working. You see, I had left her and the other girls in A.C. to keep working while I was on the road. She was my bottom lady. We talked about business and she told me that everything was going great. I hung up and I went back to getting down with the pimping at hand. Misty Rain and Lola, oh!, that was the girls' names. They both had nice tight asses. Lola was living proof that astounding asses come in all colors and Misty Rain puts the "Beauty" in Beauty and the Beast. These two white leading ladies looks came in handy down here in New Orleans. The first week was great and I had made about 10 grand. Then the shit started. I had been so busy getting money that I didn't pay that much attention to what these girls were up too. They were freaks for each other. Anyway, this one particular Saturday night around 5pm, they called a cab to go to work and about 5 hours later, my boys and I were ready to hit the stroll and collect our traps. Three hours later and I still couldn't find my ladies. I asked my boys to check with their ladies to see if they had seen them, hoping that they hadn't got picked up by the police. Parker said, "yo man! The word is that they both were in the strip club dancing."

Now I'm thinking that my trap must be on full with them in a club dancing and having fun, so me and my boys go around to the club and pay our $10.00 to get in. The place was packed and jumping, tricks and hoes everywhere.

As soon as I got a chance to talk to one of my girls I asked her what the hell was going on and where was my money. This bitch had the nerve to walk away from me. I grabbed her by the arm and pulled her back to me. At this time, the bouncer from the club came over and asked her if she had a problem. The bitch said that I was trying to rob her. Well, to make a long story short, the club gave us an ultimatum, we could leave and not come back or they were going to call the police. I don't have to tell you what we did. Now mad as hell and no ho's, I had to do something so I went back to my motel room to check my money. Damn, I only had $250.00

"I Had To Stop Her"

left after shopping the day before buying cowboy boots and stuff. You know what a pimps gonna do. I called Atlantic City and asked Becky what the week take was. She said around $20 grand and I told her to catch a plane and come to New Orleans with about $5 of the $20 that she had.

After picking her up at the airport, we went back to the motel room, showered and went out for dinner. That's when I told her about the two ho's. Anyway, we enjoyed the New Orleans night life until around 5am. Boy-o-boy what a night!

The next day, my man Tommy knocked on my door to let us know that they all were going in town for lunch, so we got dressed and caravan to downtown New Orleans for lunch at the Hyatt Hotel. White girls and black guys, you know people were gawking, talking, and wondering who the hell do these people think they are? We loved every moment of it until we got back to the motel. I will get back to that later. (Oh, you want to hear about it now?)

Okay you win!

Remember back at the hotel where everybody was looking at us? Well, some of them were the police. They knew what was going on and was going to do something about it. We were having so much fun that we never realized that they had set up surveillance on us as we were out shopping after lunch. They even followed us back to the motel and ran our tags. It must have been about 2 or 3 hours later when we all had been chillin' in our rooms when 3 to 4 police just came walking into our rooms. Because of the heat wave, we had our doors opened. They had us all go to Pimp

Charles' room since that's where the Lieutenant was. Pimp Charles had a shoe box lid laying on the dresser with about an ounce of weed in it. The Lieutenant asked Charles what it was. Charles said that it wasn't his so the Lieutenant said "well, you don't mind if I flush down the toilet?"

After flushing the weed, he came back into the room and saw that Charles had not completely unpacked one of his bags, so again the Lieutenant said, "I guess you were about to leave, right?" Of course Charles said, "Yes sir!" So the Lieutenant said we will be back and we don't want to see y'all here when we get back.

It only took us about 15 minutes before we were on the road heading back to Florida. Now you have to understand, when we were on our way to New Orleans, my buddy Lenny from Boston was the last car in our little caravan driving a new Mercedes. I was number 2 and we were doing about 80 mph when all-of-a sudden Lenny passed all of us like we were standing still. I had told the two girls that were with me that when we leave New Orleans I wanted to leave in a new Mercedes. Well, here we are leaving New Orleans in the same Cadillac that I came in and there goes Lenny passing everybody again I hate that nigger. He's too much like me. Once we crossed into Florida and stopped for gas I told the guys that I was going back to NJ. You can't let ho's run around unsupervised. They didn't know that Becky had left so we had to get back. I gassed up we started heading north to 95 North.

Those couple of days off for Becky was like a short vacation for her but she knew that as soon as we hit Atlantic City it was back to work. She knew that I wanted a new Mercedes and wanted it by the time my boys got back from Florida.

By the time we got home, we were so tired that I let her stay home after she called the other girls and went to pick up my money. The next day, I got dressed and went out to look at some Mercedes. Everything was back to normal, if you could call my life normal.

Note: **Trickology; The art of tricking someone into believing that they are getting something that they aren't** like when I was teaching my ladies how to give a blow job, now this may sound like an easy thing but it requires a certain technique. First of all, when you think about it, if a ho is giving 60 to 70 blow jobs a night, she would end up with lockjaw. So the girl has to be taught how to trick the customer into thinking that he is getting the real thing when he isn't. First the ho has the man to lie down after lowering his pants and lays with the back of her head facing him. Then she takes his penis in her hand and using her thumb and middle finger, circles his penis. Next, a condom is placed on the penis and she can do it either by having the condom in her mouth and as she lowers her head over his penis, she is actually putting the condom on or she can put it on using her fingers. Then she will use the same two fingers (thumb and middle) and circle the penis as she moves her head up and down in a jerking motion. This is to simulate using her lips. This is done with her mouth open and the penis going into but not touching the inside of her mouth. She will then use her index finger and lightly stroke the head of his penis to simulate her tongue. After about two or three minutes but usually no longer than five, he will shoot his load. This should be practiced with a sausage in order to become an expert at it.

Note: **A Bottom girl, Bottom woman or Bottom bitch is a prostitute who sits atop the hierarchy of prostitutes working for a particular pimp.** A bottom girl is usually the prostitute who has been with the pimp the longest and consistently makes the most money. Being the bottom girl gives the prostitute status and power over the other women working for her pimp; however, the bottom girl also bears many responsibilities. The bottom girl's duties are "working the track for her pimp's stead, running interference for and collecting money from the pimp's other prostitutes and looking after the pimp's affairs if the pimp was out of town, incarcerated, or otherwise unavailable". She also has the most interaction with her pimp's prostitutes, giving them "pep talks" and keeping them in the game.

CHAPTER 6
THE DOWN FALL

You know dreaming about that stuff almost made me forget the downside of this life. Although everybody was doing some kind of drug, alcohol or some other kind of dumb and crazy shit, one of the rules in our family was that no one can do drugs. That meant everyone but me, of course. I was smoking weed and drinking Courvoisier 24-7 plus a little one-on-one of cocaine. Anyway, when the guys got back from Florida, my main man, Sir Christopher called me and said to stop by his apartment because he had something to show me. Christopher being from New York, he was the pimp that had the good cocaine.

We all copped from him so that we got the real good stuff like Fish Scales (Cocaine that sparkled like fish scales) and would not get beat.

Once I got to his apartment in Egg Harbor City, I saw that Wayne, Fleetwood Danny, and Strings were there as well. I asked what the hell was going on. Christopher was in the kitchen cooking something in a pot with a jar in it. He said have a drink and a seat. I will be you in a minute. About 15 minutes later he came in the living room and put a plate on the coffee table with three haft dollar size badge rocks and without saying a word, he left and returned with four glass pipes and a big ass lighter.

What the fuck is this nigger up to? He must have lost his mind. I was about to say something when he started to tell us about the rocks. Sounding like a chemistry teacher, we were told that it was cocaine in its purest form and that it was called "free base". After showing us how to smoke it, we all tried it and ended up high as hell. We were told that this is the big thing in Florida and were going to take over the cocaine business.

Oh Shit! The brother was right. Five years later and I was still chasing that shit. It was easy for me because I had the money and my nephew Hamil was one of the biggest free base dealers around. He had a friend by the name of George Rex who was even bigger then he was. I was even able to get credit.

As I look back, just about every pimp and ho was hooked on free base. The only person that was making any money was the pusher-man (The Man with the package). Ho's were running off with whoever had the rocks and staying with them until the rocks ran out.

Pimps were running around for weeks wearing the same clothes and with the look of death on their faces.

Sweetheart, I'm tired. Let's go to bed. Oh! Did Maria or David call today? No! Ok, let me call them before I get in the shower.

As I was taking my shower, the thought of how blessed I am to have lived through all that stuff and still be here today to tell this story. Thank you, Jesus.

As we spooned together in bed, sleep over took me and in my dream state my life picked up at the point of no return. This dream allowed me to see my old life on a big 3-D movie screen with surround sound.

CHAPTER 7

"IT ALL WENT DOWN HILL FROM HERE"

It picked up the night that I turned Becky my bottom lady on to free base cocaine.

It was a cold night at about 30°, round 5:30 AM on a Saturday morning. I saw Becky standing on the corner where she usually works. As I pulled up and turned the corner I blew my horn so that she would come to the car. Once in the car, I asked her how much did she have she told me about $400 with the $800 that I had collected earlier I had about $1,200. Now keep in mind that I just left the crack house that Shirley L. had set up and I must had blown about $300 before I left to pick Becky up.

Now with $900 in my pocket I didn't want to waste any time in getting back to Shirley's place, so I placed a call to Diesel Don to order half an ounce of crack cocaine. I always got a better price from him plus he had the best shit in town. Shirley sold stuff too, but it was always cut to hell. Diesel had that real fish scale and it was always a good price especially for me. I told him that I would be coming pass in about 10 minutes and I needed that ounce. He said no problem. So with Becky in the car I went past Diesel's and picked up the package. You have to understand that none of my girls were allowed to use drugs and they never saw me doing drugs but I was so high that I didn't think. Normally, I would drop Becky off at home and go out and do my thing. But this was one night that I just didn't think, so we went past Diesel's, picked up the package and went straight to Shirley's house.

Now at Shirley's, if you bought a $50 piece you could go upstairs and smoke it. When Becky and I went in the house I told her to sit in the living room while I talked to Shirley in the kitchen.

I told Shelley about the cocaine that I had and that I wanted to take half of it and cut it to sell I would split the money 60/40 with her but after rapping about it for a while we decided that she would not sell it at her house but for a couple dollars I could smoke as much of it there that I wanted.

I took Becky upstairs to one of the bedrooms that were set up to smoke in and there were about four other people in the room. After paying $10 for my setup which consisted of a glass pipe with screens, a small cup with 151 rum and two hanger wires with cotton balls on the tip of them. I had my own lighter.

I took about a $20 rock out of the bag and placed the whole thing in my pipe, dipped the wire with the cotton on the tip into the 151 rum, lit it with my lighter and begun to smoke from the pipe. I think I pulled on the pipe for about 4 minutes until the bowl of the pipe was clear. I held it in my lungs until I couldn't hold it anymore and when I exhaled, smoke was all over the room. Everybody that was watching just could not believe their eyes. As I lay back on the sofa that was in the bedroom, Becky was looking at me like I was going to die. When I was able to speak I was high as a kite.

After Beck saw how high I was, she asked to try some too. Now if I was in my right frame of mind, I would have said hell no, but remember I was so out of it that I did not care, so I said okay. I gave her a little less than a dime piece, I held the pipe to her lips and lit the torch and told her to pull slowly, like pulling on a cigarette. After doing this, I told her to hold it in for a little while and then blow it out. We must have smoked all but a $50 rock. My lovely Becky was now hocked on crack cocaine all because of my stupid ass. I am so sorry. Dear God please forgive me.

It was now daylight outside and people were moving around in the streets going here and there.

"It All Went Down Hill from Here"

I never liked people to see me when I was high so I decided to keep smoking until nighttime came. Once it got dark outside, I decided it was time for Becky to go back to work but the poor girl was in no shape to go to work. So after smoking up the $50 that we had left, I decided to buy some from Shirley. She could not believe that we smoked up that whole ounce of cocaine.

After smoking $300 of her stuff, she put us out and said, "JB, I love you, but you need to go home, get some sleep and I'll talk to you later." Well, later did come and my pimping game was getting really fucked up. Every time that I checked my traps I took the money and went over to Shirley's. All the other pimps would be SOS (stuck on stupid) over Shirley's, so when I got there everybody was hoping to smoke with me whatever I was going to buy because they were out of money and their women haven't made any money yet. It was always I will pay you back as soon as my lady breaks luck.

We all knew each other so it was no big deal to front somebody a few hits. We all had white girls and they made money, that's how we could smoke so much.

Now it was around three or four months later that Becky's trap starting getting shorter and shorter. I wasn't on top of my game enough because of my smoking and I didn't recognize the changes in her, like one time she came home without her fur coat.

When I asked her about her coat, she claimed that a trick had stolen it. Her eyes look like the high beams of my Cadillac. I could tell that the bitch was fucked up; she made me so mad that I saw red; I was trying to think of a way to teach her a lesson.

She saw in my eyes that I was going to do something crazy, so she decided to tell me the truth about the coat. She said that she sold it for $50 piece of crack and after smoking that she wanted some more so she tricked for a $20 piece of crack and then the guy that sold it to her fucked her for the $20 and put her out, so she walked home.

Now how was I going to teach her a lesson? I told her to get naked as I went to the kitchen drawer and got an old Phillips screwdriver then to the bathroom and got a jar of Vaseline. I put the Vaseline on the handle of the screwdriver and told her to bend over. I fucked her in the ass with the handle of the screwdriver for over 5 minutes.

That's when she got diarrhea and shit was everywhere. I made her clean up all that shit and told her to get the fuck out. She came back later that morning, swearing that she would never do it again. Well, that lasted about two weeks. That's when she hit me with the big one, she was now pregnant! Was it mine or a trick's? She didn't know and neither did I.

I told her to keep working day and night. When she had the baby, it was a beautiful little coffee colored girl with blue eyes and blond hair. About seven months later I decided that I could no longer do this. She was tired and so was I. We decided that she would call her mother in Philadelphia and ask if she could come home with the baby. Her mother agreed and they came to pick her up a week later. Now I had to get myself together.

CHAPTER 8

"THIS IS WHERE MY LIFE WAS ABOUT TO TURN AROUND."

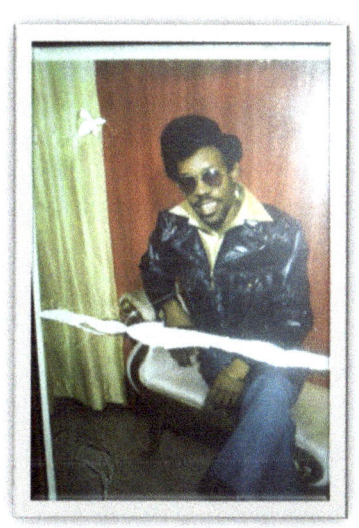

Again it was a cold winter night, the snow must've been about a foot deep as I approached my apartment door with nothing on but a sweatshirt, a pair of black dress slacks, and a pair of black gators.

I saw that the snowdrift was almost up to my door knob and I had nothing to remove it with but the thought of knowing that on the other side was heat and comfort. Wait a minute and let me back up a little bit, you see the night before I was over Shirley's place getting high for the last time at least that's what I told myself.

Anyway I must have been smoking from the time Becky left with her mother until about 9:00 AM the next morning. I had about a $50 rock left and with my head keep playing tricks on me about all the stuff that I had done and what I had turned Becky into. I decided to smoke the whole rock in one hit of the pipe.

When I finished pulling on the pipe and exhaling the smoke, my heart started to jump out of my chest. It sounded to me like the Stanley homes drum and bugle band. The room started to spend around and around all I could think of was to close my eyes and just float on, but then I heard a voice coming from nowhere. The voice was saying run, run. Just run.

So I ran downstairs and out the front door leaving everything behind. I close my eyes and again the voice said to run. So I started running as fast as I could and I ran all the way from Pleasantville to Atlantic City. Keep in mind that the snow was anywhere between 6 inches to a foot deep along the Black Horse Pike.

After reaching my apartment and knocking down the snowdrift I went aside and fell across my bed. My heart was still beating hard but not as hard as it was before. I just laid there looking up at the ceiling wanting to die.

"This is where my life was about to turn around."

I rolled over and got the telephone and called my mother. I told her that I loved her and if I never see her again that I just want her to know that I loved and appreciated her. She kept asking me what was the matter but of course I said nothing and just wanted her to know that I loved her. After hanging up from her, I tried to call my sister but got no answer. Somehow I was able to fall asleep and I had a dream about Dale and the kids and remembered how they were the only good things in my life. So I decided that I wanted to live, but I didn't know how. How do you live a life like a regular person?

CHAPTER 9

"CALIFORNIA HERE I COME"

Remembering that Dale and the kids were in California, I decided that I would go to California and dry out. I thought that I had left all my problems back in Jersey but guess what? I was the problem so therefore the problem was now in California.

Once in California, things weren't quite what I thought they would be. You see, Dale had a boyfriend, but the love that she had for me allowed me to move in with them and the kids. Do I have to tell you that this was not a happy place? They would always be arguing about me until one day I found this fine girl working at the golf course were Dale worked and of course my pimping game came in the play.

I had convinced this girl to fly back to Jersey with me and put in work. Dale got wise to what was going on so she stepped to the girl letting her know that I was her man and she better back off.

After this had happened, Dale got me a room at a weekly motel. It was basically a trick motel where people would go to get high and ho's would bring their dates. It was a 24/7 motel with action all night long.

Wouldn't you know it, I found a girl. She was nice, black and had just left her man or should I say he put her out because of her getting high on crack. One night as we were together she asked me if I wanted to try some so I acted like I had never done it before and before long all we were doing was smoking crack.

When Dale found out she was mad as hell. She said that she didn't want to see me ever again and that I could go to hell. You know me, "I said fuck it!" Well about two months later, rent not being paid, the girl I had was gone and with nowhere to go I was in the same mind state that I was in back in New Jersey.

It got to be so bad that I ended up being homeless living on a vacant lot with rats the size of baby kittens.

I remember meeting this guy named Isaac who was homeless as well. Remember readers, I had never been camping or lived on the streets or anything like that. I was a rich nigga who knew nothing about this kind of shit. Isaac was the one living on this lot so I asked him to help me.

He told me that he had an old Indian teepee tent that I could use and I said thanks but I really had no idea how to put up a tent, but with him helping me, we finally got it up. Remember, I said I'd never been camping? I didn't know that you should build a tent off the ground but the heck with it.

I keep it the way it, was on the ground. Well after smoking all night in the tent, I tried to go to sleep but outside the tent there was this weird noise and with my mind messed up on crack telling me that the noise was two rats outside my tent arguing with each other. One was a female and one was a male rat. The female rat was arguing with the male rat about being out all night drinking out of old beer cans and had come home drunk. She started chasing him around and around my tent and he ran under the tent, under me and out the other side with her right on his ass.

I remember tearing that tent down getting out of it, landing on my knees facing a chain link fence asking God to please help me out of this mess. That was my first prayer to God. I had prayed before to a pimp God that my girls would come home safe but now I was praying to a God that I had heard about at the Rescue Mission where I used to eat.

You see, in this rescue mission people from a lot of rich churches used to come and sing songs and pray for you. The night before this happened, I was at the Rescue Mission and these people that came to sing to us and one of them had asked us a question. The question was, "Can anyone tell us the difference between you and us?" People would raise their hands and say things like you have a home to go home too and we don't, you have a life and we don't, all kinds of shit like that.

I raised my hand and said, "You know God and I'm looking for him." After service was over, one of the guys stayed behind while we ate dinner. When dinner was over, they put us out of the mission. That's why I ended up on this vacant lot. The guy that stayed behind was named Rev. John Post and he stayed because he wanted to talk to me. He asked me what I meant when I said that they knew God and that I was looking for Him. I said just that! "Where is God and how can I get to know him?" John talked to me for over an hour about how God sees and knows all about us. I was wondering if God knew all the things that I had done.

John said that he had to leave but he would come back tomorrow and we could talk more. He asked if I would mind if he prayed for me and I said no problem, so he held my hand and prayed for me. I asked him to pray again for someplace for me to live. He did and then gave me some simple rules on how to pray.

The next morning after praying and sleeping, I awoke to the sounds of a trucks horn. It was the sound of some more church people who would come to the homeless with sandwiches and hot chocolate. They would also have all kinds of stuff on the back of the truck. This time they had a lot of wood with nails in them. I took all the wood and I found eight cinderblocks on the lot.

That whole day I built a one-bedroom building with a living room. I also learned to build it off the ground using the cinderblock. I found an old barbecue grill and had that for my kitchen and found an old tarp lying around the vacant lot and used it for my roof. I even built a back patio and used some old chairs that someone had thrown away. After a while, more homeless people would become residents on this lot. We all shared whatever we had to eat and sometimes even drugs. All in all it wasn't bad and we called this lot the "Dust Bowl".

CHAPTER 10

"THE DUST BOWL"

Now John was still coming around, praying and handing out tracts, talking about how good God is and what He will do for you, all kinds of stuff like that. Each time he prayed for me he would always give me $5-$20. Most of the time, I just prayed that he would give me the five dollars and be gone. He even tried to tell me that it was God that brought the wood to me and gave me the skills to build this little house.

So I decided to test John and his God. I told John that I was gonna pray to his God for a job.

Well, would you believe it? The next day John told me about a job washing cars at a new car lot. I told John that I didn't have any clothing for a job interview or a job. He just smiled and said come ride with me. We went to the Salvation Army and he bought me a shirt, dress pants, and a tie. Well, I went for the interview and got the job. John was telling me how blessed I was. The owner of the lot told me that there was a little room in the back with a full shower and I could use both anytime I want. Now I could take a shower anytime and could sleep there too.

Man-o-Man, John just would not give up. He kept at it day and night talking about God, God, and God! How God did this and how God did that, so I decided to put God to the test.

That night after work I got down on my knees and said, "God, if you're really real, I'm going to ask you for something, and if you give this to me then I know it will be from you. I would like to ask you for a new white Mercedes and just to make sure that is from you, I would like it to have a blue interior. Now God if you give me this, then I will be yours from now on.

That following weekend, the church people with the truck that had the wood on the back came by the lot once again with sandwiches. Also on back of the truck I notice a bicycle, an old white bicycle with a blue seat. I started laughing and everybody looked at me like I was crazy but I realized that God answered my prayer you see the bicycle was my Mercedes, the white one with the blue interior.

You see, John had told me that God will give you what you need and not always what you want. You see, I was homeless and what was I going to do with a new Mercedes but sleep in it.

Before long, me and that old bicycle were all over California. I could go into a store and didn't have to lock it up and no one would ever steal it.

CHAPTER 11

YO! WORLD! " I'M ON MY WAY BACK"

Not only was the job great, the guy even let me work the midnight shift as a lot guard. No one but me and these beautiful cars. There were many nights that I would take a car off the lot and joy ride around the hood all night, but there was this one night that I took a brand-new Corvette off the lot and was going through the hood when I saw one of the local crack dealers. This was one of the blocks that the Crips controlled. He was standing next to his 1964 Chevy low rider so when I pulled up in the Corvette. He was like how much you want for it? So I said $1000 and an ounce of rock cocaine, plus a ride back to the car lot. About an hour later the deal was made and it was on and popping.

The good times only lasted for about three months before I got fired and the cocaine had run out.

So here I was again back on the streets, homeless and very little money so I went back to the dust bowl and thank God my little home away from home was still available. But I was used to taking a shower everyday and getting a paycheck.

Even John was still coming to the rescue mission. The night that I saw him, he asked me what I had been up to and was I still walking with the Lord. Of course I lied and said yes. We prayed together and then he left. Afterwards, I felt really weird for lying to him. I had to do something to get my life back together so I decided to do what I do best that was pimpin, and cocaine.

My homeless friend Isaac had a good cocaine connection so we decided together that we will go down to the County building and apply for assistance. We both had received $150 worth of food stamps and a check for $300. We sold our food stamps for $75 a piece so that we would have money in our pocket. Then we put up $150 a piece from our check to buy some cocaine. We split the cocaine in half. I took my half and put a one on it, cooked it, bagged it and started to sell it.

But you know what happened, I smoked more than I sold. I think I only sold about a $20 bag of crack. I was so mad at myself for being so stupid. I was like S.O.S. (Stuck on Stupid).

The only thing to do now was to wait for my next check and do it right this time. A month later I got my check and food stamps, sold my food stamps and invested my whole check of $300 into another package. This time I did sell it and did quite well. So well, that I re-upped five or six times.

All my customers knew that I had the best package. Most of my customers were females that lived in an apartment complex called the Wilmington Arms Apartments in Compton, California. This complex was run by the Crips and the Bloods, Crips on one side and Bloods on the other.

I had all of them getting cocaine from me and being the businessman that my mind told me I was, I decided to set four of the girls up to sell from their apartments. I would give them a small package to sell and a little bit for them to smoke. If a person bought $50 worth or more, they could stay there and smoke it.

I was doing this for about a year and a half. I had gotten my own apartment, had three cars and a friend of mine from New York who owned a limousine service would drive me anywhere I wanted to go for little cocaine. Plus I had three girls tricking 24/7. The money was rolling in left and right, yeah boy! I was back on top.

Life was so good that I had forgotten all about the Lord, about John and all those other fools that was on their knees praying for something good to happen in their lives instead of going out there and getting it for themselves like I did.

(Little did I know that life was about to deal me a losing hand)

CHAPTER 12

"ANOTHER LIFE SPEED BUMP"

Things were going so good that I would be in a different motel room every night with a square girl just having some of that freaky fun and staying up three or four days at a time, paranoid as hell thinking that everybody was trying to set me up for my money.

Now my day will consist of me checking my traps from them ho's, picking up my money from the Wilmington Arms and dropping off more packages for them to sell and smoke, shopping for clothing, and freakish partying.

There was this one night that I went to pick my money up at this girl's apartment in the Wilmington Arms that was selling for me and she told me that she had fucked up my money and how sorry she was. Now this girl had good customers and never messed up my package before so I decided to give her another package. She would owe me for what she messed up and the new package plus, I gave her enough for her and her man to smoke.

The next day I went back over to our apartment and again she had messed up. Now the pimping came up in me and I told her that her and her man was going out on the streets and work to get my money selling pussy and ass. I didn't care, as long as they get me my money.

That night when I came to get them and take them to work on the stroll, she told me that she could get me my money but we would have to wait until the morning when the banks opened. I wasn't thinking very clear because of being paranoid and up all night so I said okay. We sat in her apartment and did business with me supplying her customers.

About 9:00 AM the next morning, we all got in the limousine and headed for the Sun Bank. When we got to the bank, we parked on the street instead of the parking lot and she said that she was going in to get the money. Now it was only the three of us in the limousine. You know that I wasn't going in the bank with her so I trusted her, thinking to myself if this bitch had money in the bank why would she be working for me! Anyway, I agreed so she went in the bank and about 5 minutes later I saw her.

"Another life Speed Bump"

She came running out of the bank and got in the car. As we pulled away, I asked where my money was. She lifted up her pocketbook so I snatched it from her and opened it. Man-oh-man you're not going to believe this but when I looked in her pocketbook it was stuffed with cash, $50 and $100 bills. Now of course you know all the money is mine so we went back to her apartment I gave her another package to sell and one package for them to smoke for themselves.

On the way back to my apartment, in the limousine, I counted the money and it was about $4000. I did not want them to know how shocked I was because next to the money was a note that said <u>"this is a bank robbery, give me all your money"</u>.

Now I was down with just about everything, but I'd never robbed a bank. I never even thought about it but I couldn't let them know that I was freaked out. Anyway, after counting the money and all my business completed for the day I started to think to myself with the three ho's that I still had and the four girls I had selling out of the Wilmington Arms, what if I had them all robbing banks in the daytime and selling pussy and cocaine at night? I would be a damn millionaire in a few months.

It only took me a day to put it all together. I would pick all the girls up in the limousine and we would go out and rob a least 10 banks a piece and like I said before, all monies were mine. I think this was around March when we started this and I told myself that I would quit on my birthday, July 29.

On July 27th about 8 am, I awoke from another freaking party that I had the night before and being so tired I called all the girls and told them to meet me at the Wilmington Arms. After picking them up, they all complained that they were hungry so we stopped at a Burger King on the way to rob our first bank for that day.

We went through the drive through at Burger King and ordered about $30 worth of breakfast food and as we were eating we reached the Bank of America. When the girls went into the bank to rob it, they would go to the merchant teller window which the was closest to the door and they would give the teller a note that said "this is a bank robbery fill the bag with all large bills, I have a gun, and don't press the alarm or I will shoot you."

Well, Donna was the first one to go into the bank. She wanted to go first so she took the empty Burger King bag and she was taking so long that we thought something might have happened to her but before we could check on anything she came walking out of the bank carried a bag like she was real happy with a big smile on her face. About 3 feet from the car the bag blew up.

Money flew all over the sidewalk with a whole lot of red smoke and she was screaming like she lost her mind as she ran to the car. All of a sudden the pimp ran up in me and I yelled at her to go back out there and pick up my money. People were standing at the corner waiting on the bus and here was this bitch out there scooping up money off the sidewalk that was still smoking.

Once inside the car, we put the money into an igloo cooler. We soon found out that the cooler was not airtight. Red smoke was still coming out of the cooler and I told the driver to drive away as fast as he could. The red smoke was filling up the back compartment of the limousine, so I opened the moon-roof so that the smoke could escape.

We saw something that said dye pack and so we threw it out of the window. Now, a little calmed down, we went to the next bank. Little did we know that when the police went to the Bank of America that we just robbed, people told them that they saw a black girl jump into a big black limousine after picking up some money that was smoking with red smoke and speeding away pointing in the direction that we had gone.

Well, a helicopter had spotted us and radioed it in. The police followed us as we were robbing other banks and it wasn't hard since all they had to do was follow the limousine with the red smoke coming out the top like a choo-choo train.

After robbing all the banks, with each girl doing at least 10 apiece, I dropped each one back at their apartments and I went to a motel.

With all the money spread out on the bed, I begin to count it until I got tired and threw the bed comforter over top of the money on one bed and went to sleep on the other.

Awakening earlier the next morning, I decided to go down to the doughnut shop to get some coffee and doughnuts. As I was coming back to the motel, all these guys started jumping out of bushes, running from across the street and pulling up in police cars from all directions. They threw me on the ground and one put his foot on the back of my neck screaming "don't move."

I was finally able to see that these guys were from the sheriff's department. They lifted me up and made me sit on the sidewalk as they went in my motel room and found all the money and the notes.

I was so fucked up that all I could say was don't you know who I am? I'm a rich mother fucker. Let me call my lawyer. What are you arresting me for? That's not my motel room. I was visiting a friend.

All they would tell me is that somebody wanted to talk to me. After sitting there and listening to them talk, I found out that they had set up surveillance last night across the street after following me home and planning on kicking in my door as soon as they got the word. Since I came out their boss told them to take me down.

About 20 minutes later, a black SUV pulled up and three people got out, one woman and two men all dressed in black suits with black sunglasses. They told the police to put me in the back of their SUV. As we were driving, I asked them where they were taking me and no one answered.

We ended up at the Los Angeles County Sheriff Department and at this time they had radioed in to bring the others out. I saw them bring all the girls out and they got into another SUV. We all drove until we ended up at the Los Angeles FBI headquarters.

As they were walking me in, I saw the girls locked in a large room that was all glass. We looked at each other in amazement as to what was going to happen next and what was I going to do about it.

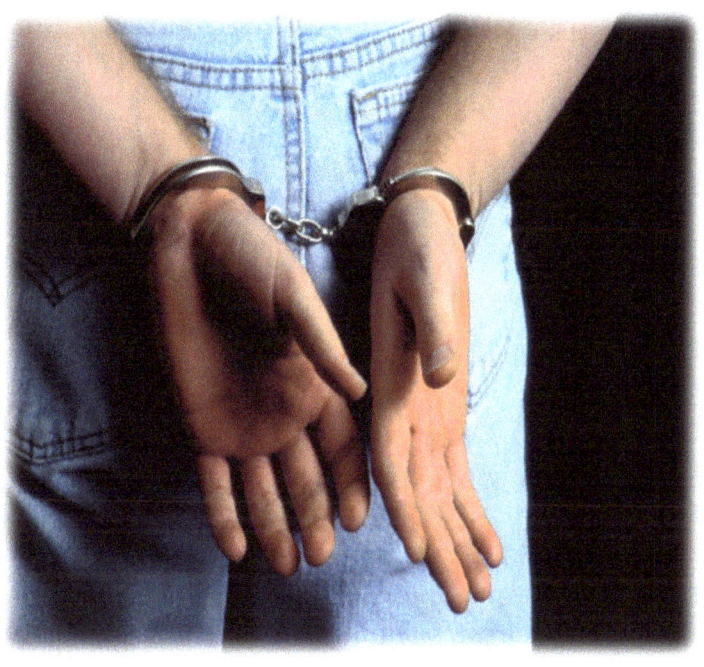

CHAPTER 13

"AWAY WE GO"

So they park my butt in a room with one door, one wooden table and three chairs, two on one side and one on the other. I must have sat there for about an hour.

Finally two people walked in and sat down in the two chairs across from me. One of them said "good morning Mr. Browne, how are you? Would you like a cup of coffee or something?" I said "hell no. Who the hell are you?" And the one who was speaking said, "I'm Agent Jones and this is Agent Smith. We're with the FBI, is there anything that we can get you?" I said "hell yeah, you can get me the hell out of here."

Agent Jones said "I don't think that will be possible." I tried everything I could think of to get these guys upset but nothing I did seemed to move them. They were so damn polite that at first I thought they were gay.

They must have interviewed me for about four hours asking me questions about different banks that were robbed. Questions like where I was on a certain date or have I ever been in a Bank of America and all I could say was "I don't know where I'm at now and as far as the Bank of America is concerned, why would I be in a bank?" Agent Jones said, Mr. Browne we're going to take a break and we will bring you something to eat.

Ten minutes later, Agent Jones walks in with a bag from Burger King. Can you believe it, Burger King! To this day I don't eat anything from Burger King. Anyway, after eating, we were at it again. Finally, I admitted robbing the banks and took the deal they offered me which was a five flat. Now, me and the girls all had got a five flat deal plus restitution.

They sent me to a federal prison called "Terminal Island" which is located in San Pedro, California. All I had to do was two years and some change before I was eligible for parole. I was in touch with the girls through the mail and we were all still cool.

This prison was pretty cool. We had the best food, a putting green and even a tennis court. A lot of inmates were celebrities. You see, the feds would send celebrity criminals from the East Coast to the West Coast to do their time. One of my fellow inmates was an old man from the Gambino crime family. They even had the police from Miami that had been robbing the drug dealers and selling it themselves. The newspapers labeled them as the "River Rats."

The papers even labeled us as the "Limousine Bandits." The newspapers always labeled you as something.

Prison wasn't bad. I was going to school, joined Toastmasters International and even became a CTM with Toastmasters International. I was working in the prison factory painting Army and Navy lockers with electrostatic paint. This is paint that comes in a powder form and is sprayed with an electrical charge. I even had a side business ironing other inmates clothing for their visits. I learned a lot of things in prison and

"Away We Go"

actually I thank God for prison. I had plenty of time to think about my life and what I was going to do when I got out.

The only fight that I had in prison was over a slice of bread. This one day in the chow line, I reached over this guy's plate to get a slice of bread and he went off screaming and yelling about how I disrespected him. He was about 280 pounds, about 6 feet 3 inches tall, all muscle and black as midnight. Now I have to fight with this fool over this damn slice of bread and it was going to take place on the basketball court after dinner.

I couldn't punk out, so I walked up to this fool, face to chest and said with the deepest voice that I could find in me, "Yo' man, I was wrong and I apologize but if you want to do this, let's do it. He said, man you must be crazy, but I like you." We became friends from that day on.

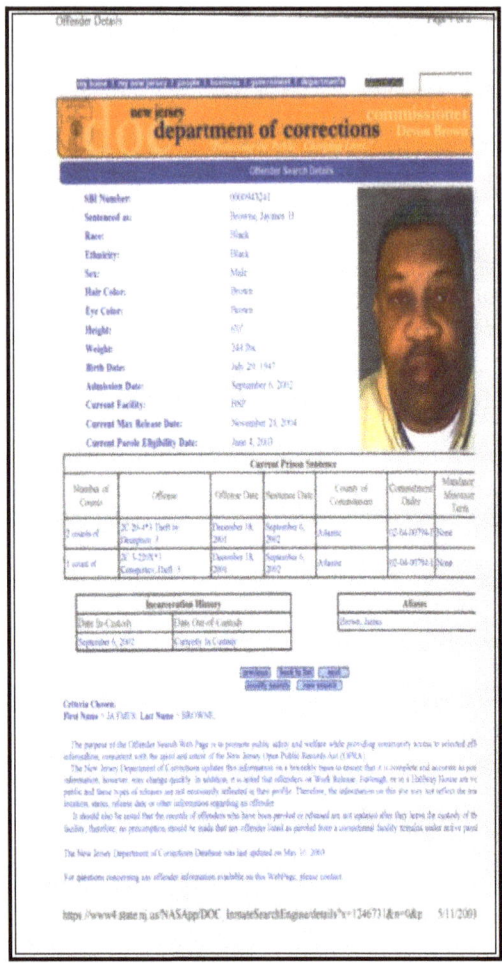

Prison was all right and everything was going my way until one day I decided to give my mother a call and see if everything was okay. Remember, I told you that I was only going to be robbing these banks and having the girls work until my birthday which is July 29 and remember we got busted on July 27th, just 2

"Away We Go"

days before I was going to stop and retire. What I didn't tell you was that I had sent my mother two boxes. One box had my clothing in it from the prison. The other box had about 2.5 million in cash which I asked her to hold on to for me until I came home. So with that in mind, these 2 1/2 years would be no problem.

But when I called her this day, she informed me that she had opened the boxes and was pretty pissed off. You see, she opened the box because she wanted to wash my clothes. When she opened the box with the money, she snapped and told me that the money was dirty money and she didn't want anything to do with it. So guess what she did? She gave it to her church! So I asked her, "If it was dirty why did she give it to the church? Was the church going to pray over it and make it clean again?" The pastor took the money and put a gold plaque on the side of a pew with her name on it. One and a half years later he retired. Do I have to tell you that I did not speak to her for the whole time that I was in prison?

That is until the last month before I was to be released on parole. I was going about my regular routine when at the end of the day I decided to go lay down. As I lay down on my bunk half-asleep half-awake, I saw the door of my room open and my father walked in.

He stood in the doorway and asked me if I had any hard candy. Keep in mind I was awake but I couldn't move. I said "no dad" and he said "Okay" and backed out of the room. As soon as he backed out of the room I was able to move again and I sat on the edge of my bed trying to figure out what had just happened.

So I lay back down again until one of the guards came to my room and said that they needed me at the Lieutenant's office. I got up and went to the Lieutenant's office where he informed me that my father had just passed away. (I forgot to tell you that I was also working in the prison chapel teaching a Bible study course that I received in the mail from Rev. Fred Prices Church.) Anyway, the Lieutenant said that he will call me in the morning and I would be able to call my mother. I couldn't sleep all night.

The next morning, the prison chaplain came to get me and we went to his office to call my mother. As I was sitting at his desk talking to my mother, she started accusing me of my father's death. You see, they had separated and he was living in Vineland, New Jersey with another woman. I would go see him, give him money and I even bought him a new car. This made him a big man in this little town and the women thought he had money. He even ended up marrying the woman who thought he had money, so therefore my mother blamed me for him leaving her.

Anyway, we started yelling back and forth to each other about everything, even about the insurance. I was screaming at the top of my lungs when the chaplain came over to me and tapped me on my shoulder. When I turned around to face him, he slapped me like I was his bitch. I jumped up from the chair and wanted to knock this fool down when all of a sudden he started hugging me and whispering in my ear to calm down. She's your mother and she's hurting. She was striking out and you have to be the punching bag for her.

All I could do was cry like a baby. This was the first time that I ever really cried. I apologized to her and told her that I loved her and that I will be home soon.

I had about 1 1/2 weeks left before I was to be released on parole when out of nowhere, one of the guards in our housing unit came up to me and told me to report to my counselor's office.

Upon arriving at my counselor's office, I knocked on his door and he told me to come in. When I entered his office, this 5'2", 350 pounds, Elvis Presley looking white guy was sitting behind a 6 foot long old oak desk. He said, "Sit down Browne," and as I sat down he opened up a folder and said, "Looks like we have some bad news for you. Your release papers from parole seem to have gotten lost and it looks like you'll be with us for about another week or so."

Man, it's a good thing people can't read your mind because I was sitting there thinking to myself, "Does this fool think that I'm in here for stealing popsicles? I should jump over this desk and fuck his ass up." I didn't want to be in this place no longer than I had to and all I know is that they better get my shit together before I fuck somebody up.

It took them about a week to get all my paperwork together and I was out, but guess what y'all? During that week, an 18-year-old Blood, Gang-Banger from Inglewood, California had just come in with 20 years on his head for a body. They put him on suicide watch because after realizing how much time he had, he tried to put his head through a brick wall.

During that extra week they gave me waiting on my paperwork, I pulled suicide watch duty and of course I had to sit and watch this guy for about a week. During the week I would bring my Bible study lessons with me and he would ask me questions about what I was doing. When I explained to him about my Bible studies, he started to get real interesting in it and wanted to know about God.

Well, to make a long story short, the day before I was to be released he had accepted the Lord in his life they also released him on the same day. Now this was unusual because anyone that was on suicide watch had to stay on it for at least 30 days but we walked out and through the yard together and it was the brightest day that I ever seen the whole time that I was in prison. Was this God at work?

The next day, the sun was shining bright as I was doing my merry-go-round and out the front gate I went carrying nothing but a big envelope with all my parole papers in it. I had given everything else away because I didn't want anything from prison. Outside the gate waiting for me was a lady named Margaret Ligon. She was the wife of Joe Ligon from the Mighty Clouds of Joy and she was my spiritual pen pal. Yes, I had turned my life over to God while I was in prison. Anyway, she drove me to the halfway house which was located in Inglewood, California.

"THE MIGHTY CLOUDS OF JOY"

CHAPTER 14

"THE LORD IS GIVING ME ANOTHER CHANCE"

Once we got to the halfway house, Margaret gave me a big hug and told me to call her if I needed anything. This halfway house was an old motel three stories high. It had about 80 or 90 efficiency rooms with three men to a room and the bunk beds had been taken apart to make three beds. There was a large square pool located in the center of the motel. This place was nice, clean and had no fences. You can sign in and out whenever you wanted to. They did have a curfew of nine o'clock, which was no problem. I was on my way to a new life.

We arrived at this place around 8:30 a.m. and most of the other guys had left for whatever reason, looking for jobs or either at their girlfriends' houses. Whatever the case, nobody was around except for staff and a few guys cleaning up. After being shown to my room, the only thing that I could think of was Kentucky Fried Chicken. I had been thinking about some fried chicken for the whole 2 1/2 weeks that I had left in prison so I decided to give Dale a call. She was living in Hawthorne, California not too far from where I was and to my surprise, she was excited to hear from me. I asked her if she would come and pick me up.

She said no problem and that she would be there in about a half-hour. When she arrived, I was sitting at a bus stop in front of the place waiting for her. She pulled up and got out of the car and started hugging and kissing me and we acted like nothing had ever happened. I asked her if she would treat me to some Kentucky Fried Chicken. She said she had a better idea and ended up taking me to Roscoe's waffles and chicken or chicken and waffles. Whatever the case, that was some good chicken.

While we were eating, I got her caught up on all the things that I had been through since I had left her, selling cocaine, robbing banks, the whole nine yards, including the death of my father while I was in prison and what happened with the telephone conversation with my mother. After paying the check, she asked me if I needed to go anyplace else. I said no, but I really should get back to the halfway house. So after dropping me off at the halfway house, we made a date for the next day that she would pick me up about 8:00 am.

After signing in at the halfway house and going through the meet and greet with some of the other parolee's, I went to my room, laid across the bed and tried to get some sleep. Needless to say, I didn't sleep at all thinking about Dale and the kids. I even thought that maybe once I got out of the halfway house, I could get a job and we could move in together and life would be great.

CHAPTER 15

"EVERYTHING THAT LOOKS GOOD...."

After dropping off the kids off at school, she picked me up and we went back to her apartment she asked me to wait in the car, when she came back she had a suitcase and I asked her what the suitcase was for. That's when she told me that it was my old clothes that I had left at her other apartment when she had put me out. We rode around for while making small talk. I asked her about the kids and that's when she hit me with the bomb.

The kids were at school and they wouldn't be home until about 3:00 PM and that she had a new boyfriend. She explained to me after my questioning her that they were together for convenience, more his convenience than hers and they were living more like roommates with benefits. She knew that he was messing around with another woman but couldn't prove it. Now I know why she was so glad to see me or so I thought. She was probably thinking that I could get her out of this situation.

After talking about her situation, I found out that she only got hooked up with him because she was angry at me and called herself getting even with me. I never called and told her that I was in prison so she believed that I just didn't want to be bothered anymore. Anyway, she was tired of her friend and wanted him gone so we had to figure out a way to get rid of him.

The kids were ages thirteen and fifteen by now and did not like her boyfriend at all. You know that kids can sense things about a person that most adults don't sense or things that they are trying to hide. As we continued to drive, I noticed that we were now on Western Avenue heading north. All of a sudden I got hungry because of all the restaurants we were passing and I asked her to pull over so that we could get a couple burgers. She said okay and we pulled into a Mexican restaurant and ordered a couple cheeseburgers and sodas. After getting back in the car, we were still headed north on Western Avenue and ended up in Griffith Park where the Observatory is located.

After parking, we got out of the car and she was acting a little strange so I asked her what was the matter. She said that she has something that she wanted talk to me about but she really didn't know how to start. I held her hand and said just start at the beginning and tell me what it is. She started to cry a little bit, you know tears in the corner of her eyes. There was a bench about 5 feet in front of us so we walked to it and sat down to eat our burgers. I said, "Dale, just tell me what the problem is and she said okay, but understand that there were a lot of things going on in my life with my mother, the kids and everything was going crazy." I said, "No problem. How can I judge you? Look where I've been (prison)."

She said that she met a guy named Charles Smith but everyone called him Chuck. On her birthday they had went out to dinner and on the way home Chuck wanted to stop past a friends' house. When they got there, he told her to wait in the car while he went to make sure that his friend was home. After about five minutes, he came back to the car to get her, took her inside, introducing her to his friend and then they proceeded into the kitchen.

There was a plate on the table with what looked like little white rocks on it and a glass pipe with some wire in it. Chuck explained to her that the pipe was used to smoke what was called "crack cocaine" and he pointed to the little white rocks. He then proceeded to break off a piece and put it in the pipe and then took a lighter and started to smoke it like it was a regular pipe.

She remembers hearing it sizzle. She said that she watched as he held the smoke in his lungs and then finally blew it out. Then next thing she knew, he was offering it to her. (Dumb Me) followed his lead and took a pull on the pipe and held it. When she finally blew it out, she felt strange, numb but good. Needless to say, that was the beginning of her addiction."

Dale went on to explain how bad things were getting with him wanting to smoke almost every night and how bad things were getting between her and the kids. They were starting to hate Chuck and were angry with her. She hardly spent any time with them or her family and it was finally starting to affect her job. She wanted out and wanted out quick.

Then she proceeded to tell me about the time when Chuck had her to come pick him up in Pasadena, California which is where he was from. He told her that he had to work late but to pick him up from his friends' house so that he didn't have to wait at the job. As he came out of the apartment and got in the car with her and the kids, some girl comes out carrying a little boy and started yelling at Chuck who said, "Just go!" Dale said that as she took off, she noticed in her rearview mirror that the girl put the child in the back of her car that was parked in front of the apartment, got in and started to follow them. They were heading back to her apartment in Hawthorne, California with this crazy girl following them at a high rate of speed up onto the Pasadena Freeway trying to cut them off and almost caused an accident a few times. Dale said that she asked Chuck who the girl was and what was going on and he said that he lives with her when he is in Pasadena and that she thinks she owns him.

After a few minutes of this high speed chase, Dale said that she pulled over and the girl pulled over behind her. Both women got out of their cars and started talking and the girl told Dale that she was married to Chuck and that the little boy was his. Even though she was in shock, Dale said that she cursed Chuck out and told him to get out of her car and that she never wanted to see him again.

All of a sudden I had the urge to wake up and go to the bathroom. When I was finished in the bathroom, I went downstairs to get something to drink. Dale had woke up and asked me to get her something too. After coming back upstairs with two bottles of water, I started telling her about the dream that I had just had and she asked me why was I dreaming about that old stuff and said that I should ask God to give me a peaceful sleep.

I lay back down on my left side and Dale started rubbing my back and I slowly fell back to sleep. This time my dream picked up two years later. Dale and I had separated again. I was off parole and I was working for a company named Duren Manufacturing and they made electronically controlled security gates. I had been working for them for about six months when one day we were installing a gate at the Sunoco Gas Company Headquarters when I saw this girl in the parking lot getting out of her car and going in to work. I would see her every day for about two weeks. On the day that we had finished installing the gate, I saw her coming out of the building with her briefcase and two other bags. She was walking with the rest of the employees heading towards the parking lot so I ran over to her car and asked her if I could help her with her bags. She looked startled at first but with my charming smile and my deep voice I got her to calm down and realize that I was not a threat. We started to talk small talk during which I asked her name and she told me that it was Romaine.

CHAPTER 16

"HERE WE GO AGAIN"

She was about 5'6" tall and 140 pounds, dressed real professional and she looked like she would definitely be high maintenance. You know the type. Anyway, she told me that she was single and lived in Cerritos, California. Her job at headquarters was supervisor of the computer help center. Anytime, when one of Sunoco's oil rigs had a problem with their computers they would call the computer help center. She was pulling down about six figures.

We started to date after about a month or so of me calling and trying to get this date. Her birthday was in a week and I knew that this was going to be my chance to show her that I was the guy for her. The only problem was that I didn't get paid until after her birthday, so I decided to ask my boss for a loan and after explaining to him why I needed it, he gave me the money. My boss gave me this job while I was still on parole and he knew my whole story. He was cool like that and I thank God for him.

Remember my friend that had the limousine company from New York? Well, I got in touch with him and ordered up a limousine and now all I had to do is find

"Here We Go Again"

a nice cheap restaurant to take her to. One of the guys that I worked with suggested a restaurant called Mid Evil Times. I said great and made reservations. I also ordered some happy birthday balloons. The day that I was supposed to pick her up I was nervous as hell. You see, I had to make a good impression on her because this girl was going to turn my life around if I played my cards right. Well, it was now time for me to get dressed and when I looked in the mirror and saw how good I looked, I had to jump back and kiss myself. I look like a Mississippi Sheriff on Election Day.

We pulled up at her apartment in this long white limousine and I had the driver to go knock on her door as I stood by the limo with balloons in my hand. She could not believe what her eyes were showing her. No one had ever taken the time out to treat her the way that I was. She hugged and kissed me as we slid into the back of the limousine while on the way to the Mid Evil Times restaurant. She asked where we were going and I told her that it would be a surprise that she would like. Keep in mind that this place was huge and it looked like a castle from the mid-evil times. When we entered, the maître d' escorted us to our seats, which was like going to a football game only with tables and in front of you there was a show that was going on where knights were jousting with each other. One knight was dressed in blue armor and the other in red armor and depending on where you were seated, you were either on the red knights' side or the blue knights' side. We were in the red knights section so we were cheering for the red knight to win and don't you know it the red knight won. Guess who was made queen for the night? You got it, Romaine was crowned queen for the night and had her picture taken. The red night on his horse rode up to her and presented her the crown from the end of his lance. With her crown on she was so excited jumping up-and-down and really getting into it shouting thank you, thank you. Thank you!

It was now time for our dinner to be served and the waiters, who were all dressed in the theme costumes, served our dinners on old wooden plates. We had ordered turkey legs. Our drinks were served in golden goblets. Oh! I forgot to mention that there were no utensils so we had to eat with our fingers and we had one big towel that we put across our laps. It was one fantastic fun night.

Once arriving at her apartment and dismissing the limousine, we entered her precious lair. It was expensively decorated so we took off our shoes at the door and our feet sank into the rich carpet. After putting her balloons and the leftovers that we had brought home on the table she turned and hugged me for about 15 minutes, kissing me all over my face and neck. She made things stand that didn't have any feet. Oh yeah! We got it on right there on the floor. We both had experienced something like we had never experienced before. I don't even know how to explain it to you. The only thing that I can say is that it was like an out of body experience.

CHAPTER 17

"WHY CAN'T I DO THE RIGHT THING"

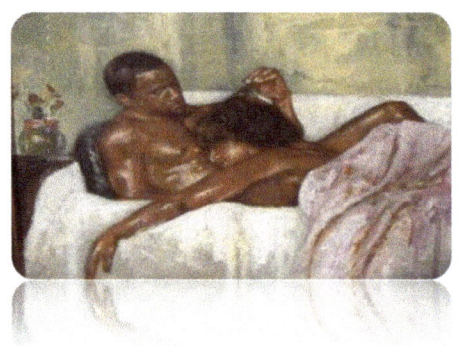

I had now moved in with Romaine and was still working. She had even allowed me to drive her car which was a Toyota Lexus. Our romantic life was like the little story of Beauty and the Beast. You see, all she asked for in the relationship was for me not to cheat on her, not lie to her and definitely no drugs. Of course I said okay but knowing all the while that there was no way I could keep my promise. You see, I was what they called a functioning addict. I was still smoking crack but was able to maintain a certain lifestyle. Nobody knew that I was using because her friends would never be in a hood where I would go to get high. So how was she ever going to find out.

One night her company sponsored a dinner at a restaurant called the Cheesecake Factory. All of her bosses and co-workers were there this night. She was to receive an award so she wanted me looking good. We went shopping and she paid for a three-piece suit that made me look like an executive. After dinner and her award ceremony, we walked around the dining room making small talk with different people and then she introduced me to her best friend.

My eyes almost popped out of my head. This girl was fine, y'all. She had long light brown hair with gold highlights hanging right below her shoulder blades. Her skin was like coffee with cream and her makeup, what little was there, looked perfect. Even her eye shadow coordinated with her dress. Romaine introduced her as Mercedes, her best friend. This was the girl that she would be on the phone with anytime she had a problem. She had told Mercedes all about we how we met, about her birthday party and even told her about the first time that we got it on in her living room.

She told Romaine how happy she was for her and how she deserved to be happy. Little did we know that the reason she really wanted to meet me was to see if I was all that Romaine bragged about. You see, she had a man that was 100% stupid and he had no idea how to handle a woman of her statue, so down deep she wanted what Romaine had if it was true.

Remember I said that I used to go to the hood to get high? Well, there was this one day I was at my boys house getting high when the doorbell rang. We were in the back room and he went to the door to answer it. We could see who was coming in the door but they couldn't see us. What I saw almost made me drop my pipe and piss myself. It was Mercedes! That's right, Mercedes. Don and I were trying to cop a $50. Why she was talking to my boy in the front room? I asked my other buddy did he know who she was getting it for and he said, "Sure, she comes by once a week to cop on the down low." The reason why they were taking so long is because she was asking him if she could smoke it there. He told her to hold on for and minute while he checked something. He came to the back room and asked us if we would mind. We agreed and she came back.

When she stepped through the door and saw me her face froze. I got up and went to hug her while whispering in her ear that everything was cool. I wouldn't say anything if she didn't. As we were smoking, she loosened up a little bit and that's when I found out that she was just another hood rat all dressed up. She was faking the funk.

You know, I had wanted to hit that ever since I met her at the dinner and now this was my chance. You see when she got high, she got loose. It was also her chance to see if all the things that Romaine told her were true. We ended up at a little motel down the street from my boys crib. I'm not going to lie, this girl rocked my world. I was given it to her every way I knew how and she kept coming back for more. With our high coming down we agreed to meet once a week and neither one of us was say anything to anybody. Romaine would probably be home in about three hours so we both had places to be. We kissed each other and left.

I got home about two hours before Romaine arrived. I had time to take a shower and get myself together. Romaine started telling me how much she missed me all day and was ready for some more of that out of body experience. As I was lying on the bed waiting for her to get out of the shower, I couldn't get Mercedes out of my mind. I was pretending to watch TV when Romaine came in from the shower and asked me to lotion her back. While rubbing in the lotion, I started to act like my stomach was hurting and that I felt a little sick. I wasn't really sick. I just didn't have the strength to give her another out of body experience. It worked this time so after dinner she got in bed and we went to sleep.

For about six months everything was going great. Romaine had bought me a used Toyota Camry. I had been driving her car because she was carpooling but now that I had my own car I was able to double down on the stuff that I was doing. Mercedes was now demanding more of my time and she was trying her best to keep Romaine from getting what she called "her stuff." Just when I thought nothing could go wrong, it did. It happened one night when all four of us went out to dinner, me and Romaine and Mercedes and her knucklehead man. Mercedes couldn't stop staring at me, blowing kisses, licking her lips and kept the conversation between her and I. Her man was so stupid that he didn't realize what was going on but of course Romaine did.

When we got home all hell broke loose. She wanted to know what was going on between Mercedes and me. Of course I lied and said nothing but she wasn't trying to hear all that. She knew something was going on and she was going to find out what it was. We had been arguing for about two hours before she called Mercedes on the phone and started questioning her. At first she lied and couldn't understand why Romaine would even think something was going on. This was the first time that I ever heard Romaine curse. She called Mercedes a bitch, a man stealing slut that couldn't get her own man and to stay away from me and her.

I told Romaine that I love her and that Mercedes wasn't my kind of woman and that she had nothing to worry about. I don't think that she believed me but things calmed down enough for us to go to bed. We slept back to back the whole night. Everything was good for a couple weeks. I didn't see Mercedes and I tried my best to put all my attention on Romaine. Until one day I went past my boys' house and Mercedes was there. She was already high when I walked in. When she saw me she jumped up, grabbed me by my arm and pulled me back outside. She tried to act like she had an attitude with me because I hadn't called her since Romaine cursed her out.

She also told me that she had put her man out and now she had her apartment all to herself. She wanted to know how much I was going buy and I told about a $50. She said, let's put ours together and then go to her apartment. Needless to say, I followed her to her apartment where she proceeded to turn on some music and close the blinds. We were sitting in her bedroom getting ready to smoke. The room smelled real nice and was richly decorated.

I felt like I was in one of those rich white ladies bedrooms that you see in a magazine. She took the first hit and then passed the pipe to me as she lay back on the bed moaning while I was hitting the pipe. She got up and started taking her clothes off. I didn't know that she was the type that liked to get naked when she was getting high.

She took another hit and started dancing to the music doing a real slow grind. All she needed was a pole. I got to tell y'all this girl was like a goddess and she had me in her trance. Hell! I took my clothes off and took another hit and started dancing with her grinding all up on that ass, turning her around and sucking on her ripe tits, pushing her back on the bed while she took another hit. While she was lying on her back, she gave me a shotgun. After holding the smoke in, I exhaled it in her pussy and of course I had to taste it and I know you can guess what happened next. We were getting it on for about three or four weeks. Every day I would meet her at my boys crib and we would end up at her apartment doing the same thing. Each day was more intense than the next. Man I was hooked on crack and her. Every time that I would have sex with Romaine I would be thinking about her. It got to the point that I couldn't have sex without a hit.

Things started to fall apart. Mercedes would call Romaine's house and when Romaine would answer the phone, Mercedes would hang up. Romaine knew it was Mercedes calling because her number would show up on the caller ID. I mean this girl would be calling 10 to 12 times a day. I kept telling Romaine that she was probably calling so that they could be friends again but of course Romaine was smarter than that. She knew that something was going on with us but she just couldn't prove anything yet.

CHAPTER 18

"FALLING ON MY FACE AGAIN"

It was now June and the weather was real nice, so nice in fact that I couldn't see myself going to work. Plus, I wanted to spend more time with Mercedes. She had quit her job at Sunoco and was now living off her savings and unemployment. So with time on my hands and no job, we were now together all day. It was like I was living two lives with two women and two apartments. I was now staying out all night and coming home when Romaine went to work. One night when I came home, Romaine was there. She had taken the day off.

When I walked in, she was cooking breakfast and asked me if I was hungry. She was real cool, no attitude. She was acting like nothing was wrong so I asked her why did she take the day off and she said that her vacation started tomorrow and she was going to fly back to the East Coast to visit her mother who lived in Philadelphia. I asked her if she wanted me to go with her. She said no because her mother was sick and she would probably be there for about two weeks.

I was thinking to myself this is great, now I get to spend more time with Mercedes. So that night I made love to Romaine like I haven't done in a long time. The next morning I took her to the Los Angeles Airport and before she boarded the plane she asked me (really she pleaded with me) to pick her up at the airport when she returned. I said okay and kissed her goodbye.

Now with Romaine out of away, Mercedes and I were at it 24/7. We didn't eat, we didn't sleep, we just freaked with each other. She was doing things to me and I was doing things to her (let your imagination go wild). The day that Romaine was to come home, she left a message on my cell phone because I wouldn't answer the call. I was too messed up to even talk. The message told me about the flight and the time that she would get in. I don't know how I made it back to Romaine's apartment but when I got there I went to turn the TV on and then I remembered that I had pawned the TV, the microwave and two of her fur coats.

I sat on the living room floor not knowing what to do. I just sat there thinking about Romaine coming home tomorrow and if she had picked up the submarine sandwich that I asked her to bring back. I must have fallen asleep because the next thing that I knew Romaine was standing over me kicking me in my side, screaming "you mother fucker. I had to catch a cab all the way from the airport and here you are butt naked laying face down on my damned carpet. What the fuck is wrong with you? Get the hell out of here. NOW! I mean it Jaymes. Get out, get out now. If you don't get out now I'll call the police. Now get the fuck out!"

While she was walking around the apartment yelling, she noticed that the TV, microwave, VCR, and that the closet door was open and two of her fur coats were also missing. She said "mother fucker, if my shit is not back in here by tomorrow, I will have your ass killed!"

I got up and got dressed the best that I could and tried to explain to her that I would take care of everything. She just said, "Get the fuck out NOW and leave the car."

Well, I left and took the car. I thought about going back to Mercedes apartment but after doing what I did to Romaine, I knew that I needed some help to get my shit together. I rode around for a while and thought that the best place for me would be a drug program.

I stopped at a motel and looked through a telephone book to see if I could find a program. The only one that was not too far away was the Salvation Army alcohol program. It was located in downtown LA on 5th Street, so I went there and signed myself in. I told them that I had an alcohol problem and they accepted me into the program.

I called Romaine the next day to let her know where I was and what I had done. The only thing that she said was, "Where's the car?" I told her that it was parked down here in the parking lot and that I was sorry but the drugs had me doing all this shit. I also told her that when I get out I was going to be a different person and I asked her if she would wait for me and give me a second chance. She said "good-bye" and hung up the phone.

Two weeks after being released from detox, I was kicked out of the program. You see after 30 days and detox they give you a job assignment. Mine was unloading the big trucks that came in with donations such as clothing, furniture and bicycles. People even donated cars. One day a truck came in and on it were about 15 pairs of brand new jeans, so I took two pair that was in my size. One of the counselors saw me and reported what I had done, so they kicked me out of the program for stealing.

Now, back on the streets in downtown LA with nowhere to go, I asked some of the other homeless people that were on the streets if there were any other programs in the area. They told me about a program called the Harbor Light Center. So I went and signed myself in. Romaine had come and picked up the car. I wasn't able to make any calls for about 30 days because of the blackout while you're in detox.

This program dealt with all the drugs, alcohol, cocaine, heroin, pills and any other drug that you can think of including marijuana. This program was really

"Falling On My Face Again"

cool. I learned a lot and the counselors were recovering addicts so they knew what you were going through. I stayed in this program for six months and then they moved me to the next phase called Harmony Hall. In this phase, you were supposed to get a job, bank account and start setting yourself up for life outside of the program. Twice a week everybody would come together at Harbor Light's for the big NA meetings.

When I would go out job searching, I would try to call Romaine and let her know how good I was doing. One day she agreed to meet me for lunch and I could tell that she was still in love with me but that she didn't trust me or should I say trust herself with me.

She explained to me that she really didn't know nothing about drugs or ever been around anybody on drugs and that she was glad that I was getting myself together and that I was also off drugs. I couldn't help but ask her what did she see in our future and she said that she didn't know but that she didn't hate me anymore. I took that as a sign that if I did the right thing, I could have her back in my life again.

Well, I found a job as a counselor at a place called People In Progress, Inc. This was a place that helped homeless people and addicts with getting jobs and housing. They even sent me to school where I graduated and became a JTPA advocate making $15 an hour. After graduating from the program, Romaine let me move back into her apartment with a real tight rein on me.

Romaine allowed me the use of the car that she had bought me because the job that I had was located in downtown LA and we lived in Cerritos, California. About two years had passed and I was still doing the right thing and going to my NA meetings. Romaine joined me at the meetings a couple of times which gave her a better insight into the world of drugs by listening to some of the addicts speak at the meetings. I was so happy that things were finally going right.

Then one night when we returned home there was a message on her telephone for me. It was from the drug program that I was on asking me if I could come down to talk with the director of the program. So, the next day on my lunch break, I went down to the program which was only about five blocks away from where I worked. That is five city blocks. When I met with the director, he shocked me by remembering who I was. He asked me to have a seat and said "Jaymes, how's things going?" I said, "Great, couldn't be better." I informed him that I was taking life one day at a time. Then he asked how work was going and I said fantastic. I also told him that I didn't know that I had such a strong feeling for helping people.

"Falling On My Face Again"

He said great, "That's what I want to talk to you about, helping people and that he had a position that had just opened up because one of the counselors moved back east and how would I like to be a counselor at this program at $20 an hour?" I almost choked trying to say yes but I informed him that I would need at least two weeks to let my other job know. He said no problem but this job is an evening job and my schedule would be 4:00 PM to 12:00 AM. I said, "Oh, well I can start tomorrow because my other job was from 7:00 AM to 3:00 PM. We shook hands and I went to their human resource department to sign the papers and I couldn't wait to tell Romaine that I had two jobs. I thought I would surprise her with the good news at dinner. I just knew that she was going be proud of me. I had already got the stuff back from the pawn shop and she was starting to trust me a little bit more. Man-o-man I couldn't wait to get home.

Now, back to my regular job after my hour long lunch break, the receptionist told me that I had people waiting. About four people were waiting to see me for an interview about a job in the Valley. Once in my office, I asked the secretary to send one back and readers you will not believe who the person was that walked in the door. Mercedes! That's right, of all the people in the world it had to be Mercedes. O-Shit!

She was just as shocked to see me as I was to see her. I asked her to have a seat while acting very professional. I know she had 1,000 questions to ask me but this wasn't the place. I signed her up for a job and told her to report to the job site tomorrow at 8:00 AM. She gave me her new phone number and I told her to call me tomorrow and let me know if she got the job. I knew that she would get it because she was overly qualified. After talking to the rest of the people that were waiting for me, it was time to go home. I couldn't get Mercedes out of my head all the way home. I kept thinking and feeling that I was cheating on Romaine once again.

After telling Romaine the good news about job, we showered and went to bed. Of course we had another one of those out of body experiences and it was great. We spooned together until she fell asleep but stupid me I couldn't get Mercedes out of my head. It was like I was holding Mercedes instead of Romaine.

CHAPTER 19
"I CAN'T DO THIS AGAIN"

It was about 10:00 am when the phone rang and of course it was Mercedes all excited about getting the job. She was so excited that she wanted to buy me lunch. Now I knew this was a bad idea but I couldn't help myself. I wanted to see her as much as she wanted to see me.

So we met in the restaurant downstairs from where I worked and man- o- man when she walked in it was like time went into slow motion. She just floated across the room looking fine as she wanted to be and she knew that she had it going on and she did.

As we set catching up on each other, she informed me that she had been clean for about a year and how all of her savings were about to dry up that's why she needed a job. She asked if Romaine and I were back together and I said that we were and that things were pretty good. I even told her about Romaine going to the NA meetings with me. She got all excited and said that she would like to meet Romaine and explained to her how much she missed her friendship. I told her that I would talk to her about it. Then she hit me with a bomb. She asked if I ever thought about her because she used to think about me all the time. I couldn't help myself and I said yes. Then she put on that big smile and I just melted. I tried to remain professional but it wasn't working. As we got up and I paid the bill, we hugged and kissed each other goodbye. She took about three steps, turned around and came back to hug me again and said thanks for the job. I will definitely repay you. All I could say was I will talk to Romaine and see about putting you two back together again.

I got home that night around 1:00 AM because I had to go to my second job. After showering and eating the dinner that Romaine had left in the microwave for me, I got in bed. Romaine wasn't really asleep. She was just laying there watching TV waiting for me to come home. I lay down next to her and started telling her about Mercedes coming into my office looking for a job. I explained to her that she got the job and to show her appreciation she treated me to lunch. I could see that she was about to get an attitude so I hugged her and tried to assure her that there was nothing to worry about. I don't think that she was buying it so I switched the conversation to how much Mercedes missed their friendship.

"What fucking friendship! I told that bitch that I never wanted to see or hear from her again." I said, "Romaine, remember what some of the people at the NA meetings would say about the things that they had done while they were on drugs especially the women. We all have done things that hurt the people that we love. It is all about forgiving. You don't have to forget what a person has done but you can forgive them. Look at me you, forgave me and I know damn well

"I Can't Do This Again"

you haven't forgotten she's trying to get her life back together but she'll have someone like you in her life like I do. I think you should give her a chance like you did for me, so just sleep on it, okay baby?"

The next morning, as we were about to leave for work, Romaine said to tell that bitch to give me a call. On the drive to work, I called Mercedes and she answered with a big hello. I told her to call Romaine, the number was the same. She said okay and that she would talk to me later because she was getting ready to go to work herself.

It was about 2:00 PM when I got a call from Mercedes telling me that she had talked to Romaine and that they were going to get together later that evening. I was going to call Romaine and ask her about their talk but changed my mind because neither one of us wanted Romaine to know that Mercedes and I were talking like that. Well, Romaine and Mercedes got to be friends again and this one night that we were getting ready to go to the NA meeting, I suggested to Romaine that she introduce Mercedes to a friend of ours that was also in recovery since he would also be at the meeting. She agreed and I know she was thinking that maybe if we introduce her to someone else she would leave me alone. Romaine wasn't taking any chances. This girl had smartened up.

When she met our friend, they hit it off and became an item. Now, Mercedes was once my bitch and she knew what we were trying to do but she was going to flip the script.

Needless to say, Mercedes and I were back together again. I wanted to kill myself for being so stupid but I couldn't help myself, believe me. Life now was in limbo driving back and forth from downtown LA to Cerritos every night got to be too much. Remember Dale? Well Dale and the kids had moved again but she still had the same phone number. I called her one day from my office to find out how her and the kids were doing and after telling me that everything was fine, I asked if it would be possible for me to spend a couple nights at her apartment because I had a second job and how hard it was to drive back and forth and that I would pay her. After explaining to her what I had been doing all these years she agreed.

"I Can't Do This Again"

Romaine really didn't like the idea but she realized how much gas it cost and she really didn't want me on the road that tired, so she agreed to it. While everything was going okay with me working two jobs, everything was okay with Romaine. Mercedes and I were kicking it on the side until this one night when I was with Mercedes she took out a $20 rock and started to smoke it and before I knew what was going on she blew me a shotgun. Well, do I have to tell you it was on and popping from that day on?

One night after leaving Mercedes, I was heading home to Romaine. I was so tired and high that I ran into a telephone pole and totaled the car. The doctors said that I had a heart attack. When Romaine came to the hospital, the doctors told her that I had a heart attack and that I had so many drugs in my system that I should have been DOA. Romaine got so pissed off that she passed out and when they revived her, she told the doctors that she wished that I had died. I knew that there was no way I could explain my way out this time. She called my job while I was in the hospital and told them about the drugs in my system and of course, both jobs fired me.

The only person that I could think of that would give me a helping hand was Dale. No matter what I went through, Dale was always there to help out. I called her from the hospital and she let me come and stay with her and the kids. I was so tired of this up-and-down life of mine that Dale and I decided that the best thing for me was to go back home to New Jersey where my family was. So Dale called my sister who was now living in Connecticut and told her about my heart attack. Dale and my sister agreed to get me a bus ticket to Connecticut because all the family would be at my sisters' house for Christmas and how happy they all would be to see me again.

The bus ride was long and cramped but when I arrived in Connecticut, my sister and mother was at the bus station to meet me. All my mother could say was, "Why don't you have any socks on?" I told her that people in California did not wear socks or underwear and she was speechless. We got to my sisters' house and it was the first time that I got to see my niece and my nephew. They were so cute and guess what? They even like me. Children can sense things in people and they knew I was a good guy.

Anyway, they had Christmas gifts for me, socks and underwear, just what I needed. You can ask my mother if you don't believe me. I stayed at my sisters' house for about a week before taking the bus back to Atlantic City and stayed at my mothers' house. After about two weeks of living with her, I realized why I left in the first place. Now don't get me wrong, my mother is a beautiful person, but living with her, now that is a different thing and that's all I'm going to say about that.

I had to figure a way out of my mother's house. Fortunately for me, I had another friend that I could always count on and her name was Diane. Now Diane used to be a model and a singer and she knew me very well. She knew me when I was a pimp, she knew me when I was on drugs and she always stood by me.

"I Can't Do This Again"

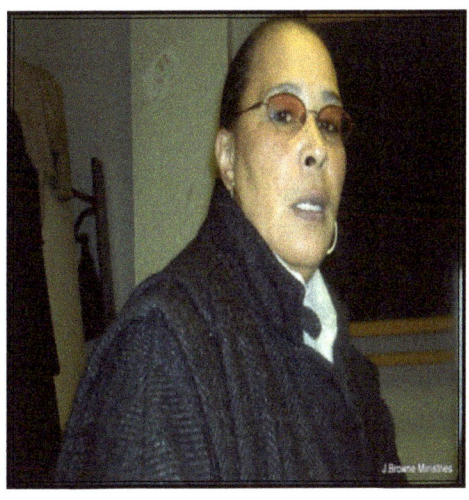

So I got Diane's number from a friend and called her. She was happy as hell to hear from me. She kept shouting, "You're alive! You're alive!" I said, "Of course I'm alive." She started to explain to me about the rumor that was going around that I had died. That the mob had killed me because I stole a kilo of cocaine from them and tried to run and they were supposed to have caught up with me and killed me. It's funny how people can create shit about you when they don't know anything. I guess it gives them something to talk about when they have no life of their own.

Anyway, after about a half an hour of chitchatting, I told her about my living conditions and how I really needed someplace else to stay. She told me that she was now staying in a two bedroom apartment in the six bedrooms apartment complex and that I can move in with her and just pay her something towards her rent.

I told her that I'd get back with her in about two weeks. You see, I had a lead on a job from my cousin Angela Burton. It was for a salespersons position at a store on Atlantic Avenue called High Five. This store sold men's hip-hop clothing and beepers.

I went for the interview with some Koreans that own about three quarters of the stores on Atlantic Avenue. I got the job and found out that I was pretty good as a salesman. Hell, I had been selling pussy, so for me it was just a different product and I became very good at it.

After my first paycheck I called Diane again and told her about the job and asked if the offer was still good about the bedroom. She said yes and I told her that I would be there later on that day.

Later on after arriving at her apartment, we were sitting at her kitchen table just small talking when I realized how great of an arrangement this was for the both of us. You see, she had gotten a little older and a lot smarter, leaving the old crowd alone and staying to herself. It looks like the only person in her life was her little grandson who she babysat for three times a week.

My bedroom was on the first floor and hers on the second. We never had sex or even played around with the idea. She was like my sister, always preaching to me and protecting me, talking to me about God and how good he is. She even tried to get me to pray with her one night.

One day when I came home from work, she was in the kitchen cooking up a big meal. I asked her what was going on and she told me that one of her cousins who just got out of jail was coming over for dinner and I asked her if she wanted me to leave for a while.

She said "No, as a matter of fact, I want you to meet him. You might be just the person to talk to him and help him get his life back together." Well to make a long story short, when he came over for dinner that night, I was surprised as hell this guy and I used to get high together. Being that Diane was a Christian we acted like we didn't know each other until after dinner when we went outside to smoke a cigarette, we started taking about the old days and catching up on who was still around and who wasn't.

Diane let him sleep on the sofa that night. The next day we went walking through the hood and the first thing that he wanted to do was go cop some blow (cocaine), so we went to Venice Park and got $250 worth of crack cocaine then we went over to the first village to visit an old girlfriend of his. She had pipes and everything else that we needed to smoke with. While I set in the kitchen and smoked they were in the bedroom smoking and getting his groove on. This went on and on for about three months, it was now around January or February and I just got my first income tax check so the first thing that I did was go out and rent a Mustang, then I went and got a ounce of rock cocaine. After I picked him up, we drove over to his girl's house in the village and asked her to call some of her girlfriends then we all drove over to a motel on the White horse Pike. I know I don't have to tell you what a party we had! After the cocaine was all gone he and his girl left to try to get some more but they never come back, so all that day me and the two girls just sat around pushing our pipes and tweaking. The next morning I took the girls home and I went

"I Can't Do This Again"

back to Diane's. She asked me where her cousin was and I told her that I didn't know. I hadn't seen him in a whole day and we hadn't heard from him in about a week until one day Diane got a call informing her that he had been shot.

The word on the street was that he had snitched on someone and they caught up with him. I felt like God was trying to tell me something. You see I could've been with him at that time and could have been killed too. God was still trying to get my attention and believe it or not that did it for me. My life was getting ready to take a big change.

The next day I got in touch with my friend Jimmy from the old days just to rap and see what was going on in his life. His live-in girlfriend, well, really the girl that he lived with named Donna answered the phone. I said hello and all the pleasantries and asked if Jimmy was in. She said no and asked what was I doing these days? I told her that I was working and trying to get my life back together and now staying with Diane which she already knew. Out of the blue, she asked me did I belong to a church I said no but I was looking for one, so she invited me to go to church with her the following Sunday with the reservation and my voice I agreed. Sunday came and we went to her church which was Shiloh Baptist Church where the preacher was Rev. James Washington and his wife Ruby was playing the Organ on this Sunday.

I don't know what came over me at the time, but while Donna and I sat in the pews next to each other listening to the music with this man preaching, it made me stand up and walk to the podium with two other people. When asked, I told somebody that I wanted to join the church and hallelujah, I became a member and Donna was happy. Everybody started hugging me and they even had a Narcotics Anonymous Program at this church. Everything seemed to be going great. Diane was super happy that I joined her church and for the first time I felt some joy. Good things were happening at this church. The preacher preached a good word and the first lady can play one heck of an organ. Oh! This was truly the good times. I loved the way the church made me feel. I love the people and the pastor seemed to always be preaching at me. He made you feel like you were somebody important it seemed like whatever you have been through he had been there too. I wanted to be just like this guy. This went on for some time until eventually the church had to move because it was an old church and needed a lot of repairs. Instead of spending money on the old church the church moved to a new location.

While plans were being made to build a new church, we moved to the Soldiers home where we held services every Sunday.

During this time, I tried to get the feeling back that I once had at the old church but for some reason my spirit remained in some sort of limbo. It was like the Lord took a holiday or something. This lasted for quite some time until finally the Lord spoke to me and said just be still, I have not forgotten you. Just be still, I got your back. Just be still and stop bugging me.

Once I took my focus off of my problems and focused on His words I started. to have a little more peace in my life. Everything seemed to be working out.

"I Can't Do This Again"

I can remember God talking to me and telling me that He's been calling me for a long time and why was I running from Him. At first I didn't quite understand but after looking back over my life, He was right. I had been running from him. So I dropped down and said God, please forgive me and let me know what it is that you want me to do and I will do it. God told me that he wanted me to go back to my brothers and sisters that were still lost in the world of darkness that I came from. Go back and bring them out using my words. I said, "Okay Lord, but how do I do it." He said, again, just be still I got you.

Finally the time came where we were able to build our new church. We were blessed with over $5 million to build our church. No more building funds and everything in the church from the new baptismal pool to the pencils on the new cherry wood tables were paid for. Our Pastor who designed the whole building, did a wonderful job. When you walked into this church, you would feel like you were walking into heaven. We had a big dedication service and as people walked in their eyes got big as doorknobs. They could not believe how beautiful this church was.

At our first Sunday service, I remember sitting in the pew next to Donna, Jimmy's girlfriend again. My brothers and sisters, I got to tell you the music ministry and choir ministry had my soul on fire. I just couldn't stop thanking the Lord. I stood up with my hands in the air running in place. I just couldn't stop thanking the Lord! Even while the preacher was preaching the message, I still kept thanking the Lord, my brothers and sisters. I was truly in the Spirit. When I came out of the Spirit, I found myself standing in front of podium telling the pastor that I wanted to become part of the ministerial staff and I wanted to be a preacher.

Well, after entering into an extreme, extensive, seeming like forever, theological study program, and passing all requirements including a trial sermon which was one of the scariest things I have ever done, I was ordained a Licensed Minister from the New Shiloh Baptist Church and Community life Center.

Man-oh-man, I was on fire for the Lord. At first I was just preaching at a service called Friday night live. This was a service that our pastor put together for multiple reasons. One of which was to give all of us ministers a chance to practice preaching the Lord's word. This, believe it or not, brought me closer to the Lord because of all the studying I had to do to prepare my sermons.

It was about a year later when one Sunday I was sitting on the pulpit listening to our pastor preach about being a bleacher preacher. (a person that tries to coach a team from the bleachers at a football game) He was telling us how to be more active get into the game to at least be part of the team.

This sermon stay with me for some time until one day as I was stopped at a red light watching a bunch of homeless people make their way to the Atlantic City Rescue Mission. That's when it hit, me the Lord had just given me a vision, I knew now why he has saved me, why He raised a thug up, why He sent me through the Lord's Boot Camp, why He had given me compassion for my fellow brothers and sisters, and why He had given me an attitude of gratitude. My dear brothers and sisters, I knew what I had to do.

So I pulled up and parked in front of the Atlantic City Rescue Mission, went inside and asked to see the director. Just to show you how God works, I had no appointment, I wasn't dressed in a business suit, no business plan, and had no idea of how to set what I was about to do up, but I trusted in the Lord.

I asked the director about coming into the mission and preaching the word of God to the brothers and sisters that were there. The director must have been touched by the Lord because when I left his office we had set up a date, time and place for me to come in and bring the word of the Lord. I was so happy and filled with the Holy Ghost that when I was leaving I just kept thanking the Lord all the way to my car. Once in my car, I started praying to the Lord, thanking Him and asking that the Holy Spirit come with me to help me do what I had to do.

I went to my pastor and informed him on all that had happened and he gave me his blessings. Our pastor is the kind of man that would not stand in the way of the Lord. He wanted all of the ministers in the church to go out into the fields and get busy, to be active in the community, not just sitting in the bleachers but get in the game. It only took a short while before the Lord and I put together a team and we were in the mission preaching His word the first Monday of every month.

The Lord truly has blessed me with everything that I need to do his work. He blessed me with a loving wife who knows and loves the Lord, a home with extra bedrooms where a weary soul can rest his head, a new car so that I can help the elderly from point A to point B, a job where I can help other brothers and sisters through their addictions, He has also blessed me with a mother, brothers and a loving sister who loves me for just being me, a church family with a pastor who doesn't mind sharing the podium, and one of the greatest gifts of all he's given me my life. Thank you Jesus!

CHAPTER 20

ARE YOU READY?

Beep, beep, beep, beep, beep, the alarm clock just went off as I rolled over to hit the button on the clock, I realized that I was wet like I had just gotten out of the shower. Dale woke up and asked me if I was all right. She thought maybe I might be sick or something because of the way that I look. I told her that I was fine and I told her about the dream that I just had. She said, "Jay, you need to pray that's nothing but Satan trying to get the best of you and that's the reason that it called the past is because that's what it is the past. I said you're right babe and I got up to take my shower and off to work I went.

Now today was Monday and I knew that I had the ministry at the Atlantic City Rescue Mission tonight, but after the dream that I had I just could not get my mind around the sermon that I had prepared. So I asked God to help me and to give the message that he wanted me to bring to the people at the Mission tonight. God being true to his word gave me the message. He told me to give my testimony and to give it from my heart with the Jay Bee touch.

When I got home from work I went straight to my office and started putting pen to paper, I must've ripped up four or five pages before it hit me" just let God lead you". Okay God, I'm trusting in you. Have your perfect way. Dale had walked in my office and asked me if I wanted any dinner and I told her no. That I was full of the Holy Spirit and just needed some time to be alone before we went to the mission. She said that she understood and left me in the presence of the Lord. My brothers and sisters, what I'm about to write now is the sermon or testimony that the Lord put on my heart to give to the brothers and sisters at the Rescue Mission.

"Hold on ya'll the Holy Spirit is speaking to me!"

Please keep in mind that everybody that is in a Rescue Mission is not an addict, they just trusted the wrong medication.

Everybody that is in a Rescue Mission is not crazy, they just trusted the wrong people.

Everybody that is in a Rescue Mission is not a bad person, they just made some bad decisions.

Everybody that is in a Rescue Mission may be your brother or sister, your mother or father or your son or daughter.

Everybody that is in a Rescue Mission may or may not know God but can they be saved? The answer

is yes, although they may not have a home of their own here on earth, but praise God they have one in heaven. Can somebody say amen?

CHAPTER 21

BACK TO THE SERMON / TESTIMONY

Back to the sermon /testimony

Prayer; Dear Heavenly Father I thank you for the blessings of today. I thank you for all that you are doing and will continue to do in my life. I thank you for my wife and I ask you Father, to look in the hearts of all of those under the sound of my voice and bless them in accordance to your will. I ask you to send the Holy Spirit to guide me in my testimony. We ask you father to bless us right now with an attitude of gratitude. All those who know the father say AMEN, and AMEN!

First, I like to thank everyone for coming out tonight, I like to thank the shepherd of this facility for letting us come in and share with you the love of God. We are J Browne Ministries and we come in the first Monday of every month. We come from different churches but we serve one GOD, and we would like for you to know that we love you even if you don't love yourself. We don't believe that you are a bad person just because you're in this place. We believe that you might have made some bad decisions and God led you to this, his refueling station. Amen!

Tonight I would like to tell you a little story that happened a long time ago.

Once upon a time in a land not far, far, away, there stood this magnificent mansion on the tallest hill in the land overlooking the valley below. This mansion was so magnificent that you could see it no matter where you were. It had two eight-foot high doors made of red oak. Once you entered through the doors, you found yourself standing in this magnificent waiting room with marble floors, two staircases leading to the second floor and in the center of this room was a 6 foot round marble table. Sitting on a 4 foot gold pedestal in the center of the table stood a 3 foot tall crystal vase. Every morning the house keepers would put fresh cut flowers into this crystal vase so that whoever walked into the house would see these beautiful flowers and how great they smelled. My brothers and sisters this house was all that.

Well, one day a strong wind came and blew the double doors open. The wind blew so hard that it knocked the crystal vase off the table. When the vase hit the marble floor, flowers and little pieces of crystal was scattered all over the floor.

The housekeeper came with a broom and dust pan to clean up the pieces of crystal and flowers. She put them into a black trash bag and tied the bag up.

She then walked out the back door of the mansion to place the bag in the dumpster that was in an alley running along the back of this mansion.

After she dumped it, she went back into the house. A short time later, a homeless person pushing a shopping cart came down the alley looking in one dumpster after another, looking for something that someone had thrown away that he might be able to use.

Well, when he reached the dumpster where the black bag was, he reached in and took the black garbage bag out. He opened it and saw all the flowers and all this broken crystal so he put the whole bag in his shopping cart and continued looking in dumpsters up and down the alley.

At the end of the day he ended up back to his little hooch where he took the black bag out of his shopping

Back to the sermon /testimony

cart and dumped the broken pieces of crystals onto his little makeshift table.

He looked into his cart again and found some crazy glue. While this homeless person is sitting at the table with the crazy glue putting the pieces of crystal back together, let's leave him there while I take you back to the beginning.

You see my brothers and sisters, that big mansion on the hill top was the world that I lived in, and that crystal vase with flowers in it well that was me sitting on high so everyone can see how beautiful I was. I thought I was all that sitting there for the whole world to gaze upon, and the wind that blew the door open was God. He's the one that blew opened the doors and knocked me off my high pedestal and broke me into little pieces. When the housekeeper had placed me in the trash and threw me out, this is just like the world throwing some good people out just because they are a little broken, a little discouraged they think that you're no good for this world. But in all of our lives, when the world has given up on us, here comes a homeless person with a shopping cart. This homeless person was Jesus Christ. He picked me up out of the trash and put me in his little shopping cart and took me back to his little hooch and with the help of crazy gluc which was the Holy Spirit and pieced me back together again,

He wiped me off, He cleaned me up, and He sat me on solid ground which was His little table.

You see when God had finished putting me back together again I didn't look anything like I used to because some of the pieces just could not be used but,

He took the good pieces and glued them back together into what you might call a Frankenstein cup. You see with the help of the Holy Spirit, he made me into a cup that he could use to drink cold water from as he was going back and forth in the alleys looking for souls that the world has thrown away.

My brothers and sisters, I need you to know that God broke me down and put me back together again for His purpose and not for my purpose and I'm here today to let somebody know that although the world has thrown you away, although they told you that you're no good, God can take your broken, torn and ripped up bodies and restore you for His purpose if you only let Him.

Won't you let God use you tonight? Will somebody say I'm tired and ask God to restore you for His purpose? As you know, God broke me down and put me back together again for His purpose and not for my purpose. Amen and amen

CHAPER 22

BEING SOMEONE THAT GOD CAN USE

Being someone that God can use has been the best thing and best decision that I have ever done in my life.

I wish I had the words to describe the feeling that I have since turning my life over to the Lord. It is a feeling that I never felt before. You see, I can truly say that the Lord is my friend, we spent time together at work, at home, we wake up together, we go to bed together and we even eat together. My brothers and sisters, I have to keep it real with you knowing the Lord and having him as your friend is just like having a regular human friend. What I mean is, the Lord and I don't always agree on everything. There are times when I don't agree with some of the things that he wants me to do but I do it anyway, there are times when I don't want to forgive a certain person but I do, there are times when I don't use the right words when I get mad with someone. Oh yes, I still get mad but I turned quickly and ask God to forgive me. You see, He is a forgiving God, one that forgives and forgets although I'm happily and blissfully married I have been known to window shop (just checking to see how God has blessed some of the feminine gender) just keeping it real with you.

MY DEAR BROTHERS AND SISTERS

By the putting of these words on paper, it was with the hope that by reading these words those of you who might be going through or know someone that might be going through something will be encouraged to seek the Lord.

I would like to say thank you to all that went out and purchased this book.

I believe a blessing has been dropped into your lives.

Prayer

Will you bow your heads and join me as we go before the throne of our God?

Father God, in Jesus name we come before you

Giving thanks and asking for your blessings in our lives.

Use this book Lord to encourage your sons and daughters.

So that the testimony of my heart will land in the fertile hearts of your children....Amen!

In Closing allow me to read Scripture

Psalms 113

Now of course you know the PSALMS are wisdom literature, Poetry

And they sound better in the KING JAMES language

But the understanding may come a little clearer in some other translations.

Let me deposit the first 9 verses from

'THE CONTEMPORARY ENGLISH BIBLE,' (PSALM 113)

Psalm 113

¹Shout praises to the LORD! Everyone who serves him, come and **praise** his name.

²Let the name of the LORD be **praised** now and forever.

³From dawn until sunset the name of the LORD deserves to be **praised.**

⁴The LORD is far above all of the nations; he is more glorious than the heavens.

⁵No one can compare with the LORD our God. His throne is high above,

⁶and he looks down to see the heavens and the earth.

⁷God lifts the poor and needy from dust and ashes, (that means from your lowest place.)

⁸and he lets them take part in ruling his people.

⁹When a wife has no children, he blesses her with some and she is happy.

My brothers and sisters, it is important for us to realize that whenever we read or study the word of God,

What we are reading in the Bible is the result of some event,

Some happening or some occurrence.

That is to say something happened in order for us to get the words of scripture on paper.

There would be no Genesis 1, had not God created the Heavens and the Earth.

There would be no 10 Commandments in Exodus 20 had not the nation of Israel lived in disobedience to God.

And the same is true of this Psalm 113, text.

The text is the result of something.

Something happened in order for us to have the words and the story of this text.

In order for us to fully understand what is going on in Psalm 113

You must at your earliest convenience, go back and read Judges 1-4

While reading the book of Judges, chapters 1-4, God began to not only speak to me,

But also to break the scripture down to my understanding...Can you say Amen?

Can I preach from the subject "CAN YOU HEAR ME NOW?"

Judges 1-4 tells of a period in which the people fell away from their forefathers in which they praise, worshiped, and served God.

Sounds much like our generation, doesn't it? In Judges 1:1, after Joshua died, the Israelites whined and complained,

Lord, who will be the first to fight for us, because there is a gang that wants to invade our stuff.

This is much like us, when we disobey God and get caught up in our sin stuff?

It is not always the big sin, for sin is sin whether you consider it big, small, medium, red, green or purple;

It is all sin in the eyes of God then we want to go before the altar and cry, Lord, what are you going to do about my mess?

God does not say to cry to Him, rending or tearing our clothes He wants us to give Him our broken hearts!

In Joel 2:13-14, NIV it reads: Rend your heart and not your garments.

Return to the LORD your God, for he is gracious and compassionate,

Slow to anger and abounding in love, and he relents from sending calamity.

Who knows? He may turn and have pity and leave behind a blessing a grain offerings and a drink offerings for the LORD your God.

Did we seek Gods will and direction before the mess?

The Word of God says in Proverbs 3:6,

"In all your ways acknowledge him, and he will make your paths straight."

If we would first come to God and seek His wisdom about a matter,

Then we would avoid the pitfall of a stubborn and disobedient spirit.

As we continue to look at Judges 1:2, the Lord responded to the children of Israel, praise or {Judah} is to go up,

For when you praise me, you shall have the land, that which you seek for.

Judah is derived from the Hebrew word, meaning Praise.

In Psalms 78:4, we will not hide them from their children, shewing to the generation to come the praises of the LORD, and his strength, and his wonderful works that he hath done.

What God was saying is that I will send my praise, my strength before you; so that you will know in and of yourself that you had nothing to do with the victory.

But you do have something to do with how you praise me and the level of your praise.

In short God was saying Praise moves me,

It empowers Me, I'm moved after the praise, not before.

Judges 5 starts off with a song, the song of Deborah.

The song was after just one of Gods much mighty deliverance for the Israelites.

The song of Deborah says, when we the people willingly offer ourselves as praise to the Lord,

It did not say offer up praise.

Yes, we should do this, but it says, when we (say it's talking about me) willingly offer ourselves (say it's talking about me AGAIN)

Then praise the Lord! God wants you and me. He wants us in obedience to His Word, His Will, and to those whom He has put over us as spiritual leaders.

He wants us to willingly offer ourselves. Then, in doing that, we give praise to the Lord.

Praise the Lord in your songs and your worship.

But we cannot offer God praise in any form if we do not willingly give ourselves unto Him,

For His service; not our service or our opinion of what His service in our lives should be.

In short, God is asking for you to willingly lay down your life, as His Son did.

For Jesus said, No man takes my life, but I willingly lay it down, and I will take it up again.

When we willingly are obedient,

That in itself is a sweet incense or fragrance that goes up before God. When we willingly do this,

Then on Sundays and Tuesdays or whatever day of the week you have bible study,

You will not have to be pumped up by someone else because you will come already pumped up, and ready not only to give to God but to give to others around you.

You are just moving from a realm of intimate worship to a corporate worship

When we, from our hearts, <u>praise</u> God and His wonderful works, or in short, when we pump His ego up.

You see I believe God has an ego,

Not like man, but one that loves to hear His children <u>praise</u> and magnify Him.

For David says that, He inhabits the praise of His people.

Isaiah 43:21, says, the people I formed for myself that they may proclaim my praise.

God loves to hear us worship and magnify and adore Him and His works.

The verse then states in Judges 5:4, that the earth shook and the heavens poured down out of the clouds.

The clouds represent His presence, His manifest presence.

The rain represents His anointing,

When the children of Israel went out again and chose other gods, war came to them and God provided not a shield or spear.

The shield and the spear represent Gods protection and divine provision.

In Psalm 34, David effectively says "Since I've been through and now that I'm on the other side of through I can confess without hesitation or reservation that I will bless the Lord at all times. His praise will always be on my lips.

What David is telling us is that there is no time.

No situation,

No circumstance when praise is inappropriate.

Put the book down for a moment and raise your hands in the air and say;

No time,

No situation,

No circumstance, when praise is inappropriate.

Ahh! What you trying to say Preacher?

What I'm trying to say is that in the good times, you praise Him.

In the bad times, Praise Him.

When you are sick…Praise Him.

When you are well…Praise Him.

When you got it…Praise Him.

When you are broke…Praise Him.

When you are up Oh yall aren't helping me! Somebody say Praise Him.

When you are down…Praise Him

There is no time,

No Situation,

No circumstance,

Nothing that you go through when you ought not to offer God Praise.

Can I preach the text tonight?

I just want you to know that there is a difference between Praise and Worship.

You may or may not know that there is differences don't you?

Praise is what we offer to God.

Praise is acts of adoration.

Which are either; vocal, visible or audible?

There is no such thing as quiet praise. If you are going to praise somebody, you better be making some noise.

That is why this same Psalm says "Make a joyful noise, anybody here ever been called crazy because of your praise?

David doesn't stop there. Can I preach the text?

David says in the fourth verse, "When I was in trouble, I sought the lord and He answered me.

He delivered me from all my fears," Verse 6 says – This poor man called and the Lord heard me. He saved me out of all my trouble

And God will do the same for you and I

If you will only praise Him,

Sometimes you have to go against tradition, what the family thinks, has always done, what is on the church program.

In other words, you may have to go against mans way of thinking and doing things, and stand on the side of the Lord.

There will be times in the natural; you will be standing alone,

Because you have chosen to step out in faith and trust and believe God. But if God is for us, who can be against us (Romans 8:31)?

Gideon did obey the Lord, but he did it in secret for fear of what everyone else would say or think of him.

My Dear Brothers and Sisters

Does any of this sound familiar in your life? I know it does in mines.

But the Word of God says that there is nothing hid that will not be revealed. David doesn't stop there.

Can I preach the text?

David says in the fourth verse, "When I was in trouble, I sought the lord and He answered me.

He delivered me from all my fears," Verse 6 says – This poor man called and the Lord heard me. He saved me out of all my troubles.

Blessed is the one who takes refuge in Him. My brothers and sisters, if you try Him, you will like Him. If you taste Him, you will like who God is.

I need to tell you that David tried praising the Lord and he liked Him. So he decided that he would get on God's side.

David knew that he could not do anything without the presence and power of God.

And I just want to leave you by letting somebody know that if you try <u>Praising</u> Him, you will like Him and you might as well try <u>praising</u> Him

Because you have tried everything else.

You tried everybody else.

You tried everything and it did not work.

How many more folk can you sleep with?

How much more crack can you smoke?

How much more liquor can you drink?

How many more prayer lines, you got to get in?

How many more books you got to read,

Before you realize that once you start praising and giving it over to God?

Oh, someone knows what I'm talking about.

But is there a witness reading this book who knows that I went to the Lord after I tried everything else and I finally found that God was the answer that I was looking for.

David had to confess. He said, "My praising may look like I'm crazy,

My Praising may look like I've lost my mind, but let me tell ya'll something,

In Praising the Lord, He heard me, I tasted Him,

My Dear Brothers and Sisters

I ingested Him, I got Him inside of me Now that He is in me I will always praise Him,

I will bless Him,

I will dance for Him, say yes!

And this is the lesson of this book that when God brings us out, you ought to start praising Him. Confessing and witnessing that I know I didn't do this myself.

I could have only done this with the help and the power and presence of God.

When you are finished reading this book STAND UP ON YOUR FEET, raise your hands in the air and try to replace YOUR PRIDE, with praising

In closing I have one question:

"CAN YOU HEAR GOD NOW?"

Note: please pray for me for I am still a work in progress love you all and thanks for buying this book I pray that it has blessed and encourage you....Rev. Jaymes Browne

A special gift for buying this book
They say that the game is to be sold and not told,
but because you're my special friends and my
brothers and sisters in Christ, I will tell you about
his game.

Oh, By the Way he does exist!

My Dear Brothers and Sisters

Nobody likes to admit that he has been conned. But your Bible warns that Satan wants to con you out of your most precious possession. Do you recognize Satan's greatest deceptions—and how you can avoid them?

Our world is filled with con artists, liars and thieves who seek to defraud us. But the Bible warns us about the greatest deceiver of all—Satan the Devil. Are you aware of his tactics? Are you prepared to avoid his schemes, or could you fall victim to his deceptions?

We have all heard stories about crooked salesmen who do their best to defraud senior citizens and rob them of their life's savings. We know about corrupt businessmen who use false accounting to cheat investors and avoid taxes. You may have experienced thieves breaking into your home and robbing you of your possessions.

But did you know that there is a thief who wants to rob you of the most valuable possession of all—your eternal life and your future as a child of God? This thief works through deceptive practices, from selfish vanity to pride to dangerous occultism, seeking to turn people away from the truth and from the way of life that will bring true happiness—God's way.

Your Bible warns of a Great Spirit war that will take place in the future—actually in the very near future. Many of you reading this article will be alive during that traumatic time. But notice this amazing statement: "So the great dragon was cast out, that serpent of old, called the Devil and Satan, who deceives the whole world; he was cast to the earth, and his angels were cast out with him" (Revelation 12:9).

Read that carefully. Satan, the devil, deceives the whole world! That means the people of every nation. That means you and me. I have been deceived. You have been deceived. But, thankfully, God calls us out of this world's deception, through the true Jesus Christ of the Bible!

Do you think that because you are a religious person, you cannot be deceived? Jesus revealed that one of the most pervasive forms of deception is found in religious practice. And the Bible reveals who is behind many religious deceptions. Do you know who? The Apostle Paul warns the Corinthians against false ministers: "For such are false apostles, deceitful workers, transforming themselves into apostles of Christ. And no wonder! For Satan himself transforms himself into an angel of light. Therefore it is no great thing if his ministers also transform themselves into ministers of righteousness, whose end will be according to their works" (2 Corinthians 11:13–15).

Yes, Satan has many strategies, schemes, and devices to deceive us. Some unknowingly worship him as an "angel of light" while others look to him through séances, tarot cards, channeling and astrology. Millions of people dabble in the occult and seek answers from soothsayers and mystics. These dark practices are deceptive, and most who call themselves Christians can recognize blatant satanic influence. But Satan also has many other more subtle schemes.

The Apostle Paul, encouraging forgiveness for a repentant sinner, went on to say, "Lest Satan should take advantage of us; for we are not ignorant of his devices" (2 Corinthians 2:11). Or, as the NIV puts it: "For we are not unaware of his schemes."

How can you tell the difference between truth and error? The Bible gives us the answers. Jesus prayed, concerning His disciples, "Sanctify them by your truth. Your word is truth" (John 17:17). Yes, the word of God, the Bible, is truth! Yet Satan can even deceive religious people. He often appears deceptively as an angel of light. He uses counterfeit ministers who appear genuine, but are actually fraudulent deceivers.

As Christians, we need to be aware of Satan's schemes, or devices. In this article, we will briefly discuss seven of his most serious deceptions, which he uses to ruin people and draw them away from God.

Deception 1: False Doctrine

Where do we find godly doctrine or teaching? Jesus said, "And you shall know the truth, and the truth shall make you free" (John 8:32). Truth is revealed in the Bible, but we must also practice the truth. Jesus said in the previous verse, "If you abide in My word, you are My disciples indeed" (v. 31).

Sadly, the majority will not practice the truth. The Apostle Paul prophesied that some "religious" people would seek teachers to preach what they want to hear, rather than the truth of the Bible. The Apostle Paul exhorted the young evangelist Timothy: "Preach the word! Be ready in season and out of season. Convince, rebuke, exhort, with all longsuffering and teaching. For the time will come when they will not endure sound doctrine, but according to their own desires, because they have itching ears, they will heap up for themselves teachers; and they will turn their ears away from the truth, and be turned aside to fables" (2 Timothy 4:2–4).

Are you willing to be guided and corrected by the Bible? Or will you be turned aside to fables? One of the major errors of professing Christianity is the practice, by some, of pagan traditions. For more on this vital topic, read Douglas S. Winnail's article "The Pagan Revival" on page 22 of this issue.

Many do not realize that Easter eggs are a pagan symbol of fertility. Decorated trees, holly wreaths, and mistletoe were pagan traditions. December 25 was celebrated as *the birth of Mithras, the sun god; it was not the date of Jesus' birth. Should Christians observe Valentine's Day? In 496ad, Pope Gelasius I established the Feast of St. Valentine on February 14. Previously, since the days of ancient Rome, young lovers had often observed the Lupercalia—the feast of Lupercus, a fertility god—on February 15. Even in ancient Greece, mid-February was associated with love and fertility; the Greek month of Gamelion, ending in mid-February, was associated with the marriage of the gods Zeus and Hera.*

The historian Will Durant gave this analysis: "Christianity did not destroy paganism; it adopted it. The Greek mind, dying, came to a transmigrated life in the theology and liturgy of the church; the Greek language, having reigned for centuries over philosophy, became the vehicle of Christian literature and ritual; the Greek mysteries passed down into the impressive mystery of the Mass. Other pagan cultures contributed to the syncretist result.… Christianity was the last creation of the ancient pagan world" (The Story of Civilization, pp. 595, 599).

Are you practicing pagan traditions in the name of Christianity? Remember Jesus' warning to the Pharisees and scribes concerning certain religious customs. He warned them, "All too well you reject the commandment of God, and that you may keep your tradition" (Mark 7:9).

The book of Revelation warns us about one of the most pervasive deceptions. The Apostle John saw in vision the famous four horsemen of the Apocalypse. He wrote: "And I looked, and behold, a white horse. He who sat on it had a bow; and a crown was given to him, and he went out conquering and to conquer" (Revelation 6:2). As we have pointed out in previous articles, the true Revelator is Jesus Christ. He reveals the meaning of this white horse and its rider. Jesus described that the white horse symbolizes false religion—including those who falsely claim to come in Christ's name: "And Jesus answered and said to them: 'Take heed that no one deceives you. For many will come in My name, saying, "I am the Christ," and will deceive many'" (Matthew 24:4–5).

Yes, Jesus predicted that many would use His name and "deceive many." In verse 24, Jesus states that "false christs and false prophets will rise and show great signs and wonders to deceive, if possible, even the elect." Will you be deceived?

The Devil, Satan, has deceived the whole world. Those whom he deceives he holds captive. You can read about that in 2 Timothy 2:26. We must all be on guard against the devil's deceptions; like the Apostle Paul, we must not be unaware of his schemes.

Deception 2: Lust

Human nature is filled with vanity, jealousy, greed, and lust. Satan can take advantage of that tendency and weakness in all of us. He sends temptation through the media—movies, television, magazines and the Internet—and through carnal and covetous individuals.

The Apostle Paul warned married couples not to deprive one another from sexual relations. Otherwise, Satan could take advantage of our carnal nature. "Do not deprive one another except with consent for a time, that you may give yourselves to fasting and prayer; and come together again so that Satan does not tempt you because of your lack of self-control" (1 Corinthians 7:5).

In our modern age, sexual temptations are all around us. So, the Apostle Paul advised those who might lack self-control, "Nevertheless, because of sexual immorality, let each man have his own wife, and let each woman have her own husband" (1 Corinthians 7:2).

We need to understand that lust, greed and covetousness are sin. The tenth commandment states: "You shall not covet your neighbor's house; you shall not covet your neighbor's wife, nor his male servant, nor his female servant, nor his ox, nor his donkey, nor anything that is your neighbor's" (Exodus 20:17).

Instead of coveting, be thankful for all the blessings God has given you. After all, God promises to provide all your godly needs. That promise is in Philippians 4:19. We need to understand that covetousness is a form of idolatry. We can desire a person, position or possession so strongly that it becomes an idol to us. Remember this admonition: "Therefore put to death your members which are on the earth: fornication, uncleanness, passion, evil desire, and covetousness, which is idolatry" (Colossians 3:5).

We need to pray, as Jesus taught us, "And do not lead us into temptation, but deliver us from the evil one. For Yours is the kingdom and the power and the glory forever. Amen" (Matthew 6:13).

Deception 3: Pride, Vanity and Arrogance

Selfishness and egotism are part and parcel of human nature. We like to feel important. That desire can lead to deception. The Apostle Paul instructed Timothy concerning the ordination of a bishop, or an overseer. He wrote that such a candidate should be "not a novice, lest being puffed up with pride he fall into the same condemnation as the devil. Moreover he must have a good testimony among those who are outside, lest he fall into reproach and the snare of the devil" (1 Timothy 3:6–7).

Do you let pride and vanity guide your thinking and behavior? If so, you can be deceived. You can be snared by the devil. How do you counteract self-centeredness and vanity? The Apostle James wrote: "Humble yourselves in the sight of the Lord, and He will lift you up" (James 4:10).

Remember the biblical examples of those who cultivated pride, and did not give glory to God? King Herod allowed himself to be worshipped as a god! He cultivated vanity and arrogance. And what happened to him? "So on a set day Herod arrayed in royal apparel sat on his throne and gave an oration to them. And the people kept shouting, 'The voice of a god and not of a man!' Then immediately an angel of the Lord struck him, because he did not give glory to God. And he was eaten by worms and died. But the word of God grew and multiplied" (Acts 12:21–24).

Another king, who had to learn lessons the hard way, was King Nebuchadnezzar. When he neglected to take the Prophet Daniel's advice to repent, God took Nebuchadnezzar's kingdom away from him. And King Nebuchadnezzar lived like an animal for seven years, until he learned his lesson. You can read about that in Daniel 4.

We need to be on guard against pride. When God blesses you, give Him the glory. As Paul wrote, "He who glories, let him glory in the Lord" (1 Corinthians 1:31).

Deception 4: Lying

There is a classic example of lying in the New Testament. Members of the early Christian Church donated property and funds to help fellow Christians. However, one individuul named Ananias, committed fraud. He claimed to have given all of the proceeds to the Church, but held back some of the funds. He lied to the Apostle Peter. We read: "But a certain man named Ananias, with Sapphira his wife, sold a possession. And he kept back part of the proceeds, his wife also being aware of it, and brought a certain part and laid it at the apostles' feet. But Peter said, 'Ananias, why has Satan filled your heart to lie to the Holy Spirit and keep back part of the price of the land for yourself? While it remained, was it not your own? And after it was sold, was it not in your own control? Why have you conceived this thing in your heart? You have not lied to men but to God.' Then Ananias, hearing these words, fell down and breathed his last. So great fear came upon all those who heard these things" (Acts 5:1–5). Sapphira came to Peter later. She lied, and she experienced the same judgment as her husband. She died on the spot! We need to understand. Satan is the father of lies, as it states in John 8:44. So, examine yourself. Monitor your communications. Do you shade the truth? Or, do you simply lie? Do not let Satan take advantage of you, as he did with Ananias and Sapphira. Remember the ninth commandment states: "You shall not bear false witness against your neighbor" (Exodus 20:16). And we must also realize that we can live a lie. Too many professing Christians are doing just that! As Scripture warns us, "He who says, 'I know Him,' and does not keep His commandments, is a liar, and the truth is not in him" (1 John 2:4).

Ask God to help you speak the truth and live the truth!

Deception 5: False Dreams, Visions and "Miracles"

How many times have individuals told me about dreams or visions that were obviously Satan-inspired? Some thought they had seen Jesus. He supposedly appeared to them wearing the long hair with which He is commonly pictured in our society. But the Jesus of the Bible did not have long hair. Paul wrote: "Doth not even nature itself teach you that if a man has long hair, it is a shame unto him?" (1 Corinthians 11:14, KJV). Jesus escaped out of crowds on several occasions because He looked like the average Jew of His day. Do not be deceived by dreams, visions, or appealing messages. The Apostle John wrote: "Beloved, do not believe every spirit, but test the spirits, whether they are of God; because many false prophets have gone out into the world" (1 John 4:1).

The occult appeals to many people. Some try to contact their deceased relatives through mediums. Children read Harry Potter books and become fascinated with the occult. Satanic video games are popular. You need to educate your children on the dangers of the occult, satanic activities and other demonic influences. God Almighty condemns witchcraft and sorcery. He tells us, "For all who do these things are an abomination to the Lord" (Deuteronomy 18:12). Be sure to read Deuteronomy 18:9–14 and Galatians 5:20 in this regard.

Satan will use dreams, visions and "miracles" to deceive people. The book of Revelation describes the great false prophet who will soon rise on the world scene. Be sure to read this in your own Bible. "Then I saw another beast coming up out of the earth, and he had two horns like a lamb [a counterfeit of Christ] and spoke like a dragon. And he exercises all the authority of the first beast in his presence, and causes the earth and those who dwell in it to worship the first beast, whose deadly wound was healed. He performs great signs, so that he even makes fire come down from heaven on the earth in the sight of men. And he deceives those who dwell on the earth by those signs which he was granted to do in the sight of the beast, telling those who dwell on the earth to make an image to the beast who was wounded by the sword and lived" (Revelation 13:11–14).

Do not be deceived! False religious leaders will perform great signs and miracles. Be sure that you test all such leaders with the Bible, the word of God. That is why we say in Tomorrow's World magazine, and on the Tomorrow's World telecast, "Don't believe us; believe your Bible!" As Scripture says, "To the law and to the testimony! If they do not speak according to this word, it is because there is no light in them" (Isaiah 8:20).

We can all look forward to the day when Satan the Devil will be cast into the bottomless pit for a thousand years. You can read about that in Revelation 20. In the meantime, we must remain watchful and on guard.

Deception 6: Bitterness

If we are not careful to watch our feelings, we can become bitter. Perhaps someone offends us. Then the hurt feeling turns into a grudge. Then we start thinking about revenge. If such feelings are nursed and encouraged, they can turn into hate. Then, that hate can turn into bitterness. Christians need to identify and overcome any feelings of hate and bitterness. Notice this instruction: "Pursue peace with all people, and holiness, without which no one will see the Lord: looking diligently lest anyone fall short of the grace of God; lest any root of bitterness springing up cause trouble, and by this many become defiled" (Hebrews 12:14–15).

Such bitterness can even lead to the unpardonable sin. How can we counteract those feelings? Simply by following Jesus Christ's instructions! He taught us: "But I say to you, love your enemies, bless those who curse you, do good to those who hate you, and pray for those who spitefully use you and persecute you, that you may be sons of your Father in heaven; for He makes His sun rise on the evil and on the good, and sends rain on the just and on the unjust" (Matthew 5:44–45).

Even professing Christians sometimes fall into the trap of plotting revenge for some offense or injustice. God warns us against that attitude: "Do not say, 'I will recompense evil'; wait for the Lord, and He will save you" (Proverbs 20:22). Our Lord and Savior set the example, that "when He was reviled, did not revile in return; when He suffered, He did not threaten, but committed Himself to Him who judges righteously" (1 Peter 2:23).

Pray for God's intervention—that He will execute His righteous judgment. He will execute vengeance, if it is divinely warranted. Christians should not take vengeance into their own hands and succumb to Satan's attitude of hate. Scripture warns us: "For we know Him who said, 'Vengeance is Mine; I will repay,' says the Lord. And again, 'The Lord will judge His people.' It is a fearful thing to fall into the hands of the living God" (Hebrews 10:30–31).

Christians need to pray for their enemies. Bless those who curse you. That is the Christian way! That is how we can overcome Satan's infectious attitude of hate and bitterness.

Deception 7: Lack of Faith

When Satan attacked him, the patriarch Job remained faithful to God—and learned vital spiritual lessons. At one point, Job said: "For the thing I greatly feared has come upon me, and what I dreaded has happened to me" (Job 3:25). In our modern language, we might call Job's experience a "self-fulfilling prophecy."

As Christians, we must face our fears with faith, and must pray for God's protection and intervention. When we study the Bible, and we believe God's promises, He gives us faith. Scripture reminds us, "So then faith comes by hearing, and hearing by the word of God" (Romans 10:17).

Lack of faith opens us to Satanic deceptions. The book of Hebrews recounts the faithlessness of those ancient Israelites who lacked faith and trust in God. We need to learn from their hardness of heart, and avoid it in our own lives. "Beware, brethren, lest there be in any of you an evil heart of unbelief in departing from the living God; but exhort one another daily, while it is called 'Today,' lest any of you be hardened through the deceitfulness of sin" (Hebrews 3:12–13).

Those who lack faith in Christ, and who persist in trusting Satan, will ultimately be destroyed. "But the cowardly, unbelieving, abominable, murderers, sexually immoral, sorcerors, idolaters, and all liars shall have their part in the lake which burns with fire and brimstone, which is the second death" (Revelation 21:8). Thankfully, there is also good news for those who have faith and avoid Satan's deceptions. "He who overcomes shall inherit all things, and I will be his God and he shall be My son" (v. 7).

God wants you to be His faithful and trusting son or daughter, through Jesus Christ, our Lord. He will give you His faith, if you turn to Him with your whole heart. In the meantime, arm yourself with spiritual knowledge. Avoid self-deception. Avoid the world's deceptions. And avoid Satan's deceptions. As the Apostle Paul reminded us, Christians are not ignorant of Satan's devices. As regular readers of this magazine know, Bible prophecy foretells of a great future false religious system, inspired by Satan that will influence billions of people all over the earth. By staying close to the true God, you can avoid satanic deception. Do not let yourself be deceived! Amen!

Lightning Source UK Ltd.
Milton Keynes UK
UKHW020654141221
395606UK00006B/207